THE NATIONAL GALLERY OF SCOTLAND

AN ARCHITECTURAL AND DECORATIVE HISTORY

THE NATIONAL GALLERY OF SCOTLAND

AN ARCHITECTURAL AND DECORATIVE HISTORY

Ian Gow and Timothy Clifford

ISBN 0 903148 82 x

Published by the Trustees of the National Galleries of Scotland
Designed by Cinamon and Kitzinger, London
Typeset by Rowland Phototypesetting, London
Printed in the Netherlands by Lecturis bv., Eindhoven

PHOTOGRAPHIC CREDITS : Figure illustrations 1, 2, 3, 12, 17 and 19 are reproduced
by permission of the Royal Commission on the Ancient and Historical Monuments
of Scotland, figure 5 by permission of Bourne Fine Art, Edinburgh, figures 6, 7, 8, 9,
10, 11, 13, 14 and 23 by permission of Edinburgh University Library, figure 18
by permission of Mr Ian Gow, figures 20 and 28 by permission of the Royal Scottish
Academy, figure 26 by permission of the Trustees of Sir John Soane's
Museum, London, and figure 27 by permission of the Trustees of the Victoria and
Albert Museum. All other objects illustrated are the property of the National
Galleries of Scotland.

Colour photography by Antonia Reeve.

CONTENTS

ACKNOWLEDGEMENTS

The authors particularly wish to thank the staffs of the Royal Commission on the Ancient and Historical Monuments of Scotland, the Manuscripts Department of the National Library of Scotland, the Scottish Record Office and the Special Collections Department of Edinburgh University Library for their help and unfailing courtesy, as well as the following friends and colleagues for their assistance and advice: Janis Adams, Duncan Bull, David Blisset, Ian Caldwell, Michael Clarke, Dr Lindsay Errington, John Gifford, Alan Gosling, Ierne Grant, James Holloway, Hugh Macandrew, Shona McGaw, John Murdoch, Fiona Pearson, John Pinkerton, Joe Rock, Margaret Robertson, Trish Slater, Helen Smailes, Sara Stevenson, William Terrell, Meta Viles, Giles Waterfield and Julie Williams.

The text has been efficiently typed by Sheila Scott and Lilian Hamilton. The publication has been edited by Michael Clarke. Finally the authors would like to record their appreciation of each other's ideas and encouragement in their joint exploration of the history of Playfair's masterpiece.

FOREWORD

Over the last year the National Gallery of Scotland has been transformed out of all recognition, and is now close to the splendid appearance it had when it opened in 1859.

The transformation has come about from a variety of reasons. Firstly, our Director, Timothy Clifford, was ambitious to restore these rooms to their former splendour, at the same time hanging many more pictures according to the traditional manner. Secondly, the National Galleries had the benefit of the meticulous research work on the original architect, W. H. Playfair, and his interior decorator, D. R. Hay, which was being carried out by Ian Gow of the National Monuments Record of Scotland. The actual scheme could not have progressed without the financial support of the Scottish Education Department, while much of the refurbishing has been paid for directly by the Patrons of the National Galleries of Scotland, or, through their efforts, by the sponsorship of John Menzies plc and TSB Scotland, with the assistance of BSIS awards administered by ABSA.

The reconstruction and redecoration has been undertaken by a team led by the PSA project architect Ian Caldwell, ably assisted by Phil Gibbon of the Crown Suppliers, while the main contractors were Peter Walker and Son. We are grateful to all of them for their reliability, unfailing enthusiasm, and sense of quality. The scheme could not have been realised so effectively had it not been for the contribution of Michael Clarke, Keeper of the National Gallery, who supervised many of these activities and oversaw the hanging of the pictures.

This publication by Gow and Clifford marks the third stage of the present scheme of redecoration and rehanging, which is scheduled to re-open for the Edinburgh International Festival of 1988. It is hoped that the fourth, and final, stage will be completed next year, which will include the entrance hall, gallery above, cloakroom, lift, and new bookshop.

This 'new look', or perhaps 'old look', of the National Gallery has come about using relatively little money but a good deal of courage and imagination. As a result of this transformation, both the Playfair building and the collection of master paintings belonging to Scotland can now be perceived to be of supreme quality. The pictures and sculptures are also more accessible to the public, and we hope that they will derive pleasure and inspiration from them.

ANGUS GROSSART
Chairman of the Trustees of the National Galleries of Scotland
Edinburgh, August 1988

1. William Henry Playfair (1790-1857). Oil by
Sir John Watson Gordon (1788-1864)

[I]
THE NORTHERN ATHENIAN TEMPLE OF THE ARTS

Ian Gow

INTRODUCTION

On the 30th August 1850, the cream of Scottish society gathered on the Earthen Mound above the Edinburgh-Glasgow Railway Tunnel, to witness the laying of the foundation stone of the National Gallery by Prince Albert. It was a day of national celebration and heaven-sent perfect weather. The company had been issued with a lithograph perspective of the new building whose noble Grecian porticos were to replace the squalid wooden huts of Wombwell's Menagerie which had disfigured the site for many years. The ceremony coincided with Queen Victoria's return to the Palace of her Stewart ancestors at Holyrood the evening before. By electing to remain within its 'ancient walls' that morning, leaving the full limelight to her Consort, it was deemed that she was paying the Scots a great compliment. The Prince placed a bottle containing the signatures of most of those present, and the usual souvenirs, in a cavity within the stone which he then sealed 'amid the most enthusiastic cheering'. The mortar was offered on a service-board held by the architect, William Henry Playfair (1790-1857) [Fig. 1]. Sir John Watson Gordon, President of the Royal Scottish Academy, which had been promised accommodation inside the Gallery, then applied a ceremonial level to the stone, which was finally tapped into place with a mallet offered by Sir William Gibson Craig, Lord of the Treasury; the Treasury was paying the bill. The Prince gave a moving speech in which he hailed the building as a 'Temple erected to the Fine Arts'. In spite of the 'immense concourse of people', the proceedings were characterised by 'the most perfect order'. The only person in the whole of Scotland who held any misgivings amid the general jubilation was the Duke of Atholl, who felt that Prince Albert had failed to appreciate the esoteric significance of the Masonic ritual.

United through this common purpose, it is surprising to discover that many of those present, who were officially charged with the artistic development of Scotland, had just emerged from a series of unseemly squabbles which might have been more appropriate to Wombwell's Menagerie than the lofty new purpose the Mound was to serve. Sole credit for rallying the combatants behind this cause lay with Sir John Shaw Lefevre, the civil servant who had been despatched from London in 1847 to advise the Government on a solution, since the quarrels were seriously impeding the progress of art. When Playfair was asked to draw up his contract drawings for the new building after five years of abortive schemes and arguments, he ruefully reflected:

'So I begin to hope that I have nothing now to contend with but architectural difficulties which are so much more easily dealt with than the passions and intrigues of men. How smooth the affairs of the world might be carried on were it not for such impediments.

Prince Albert approached the Mound through the Royal Institution building [Fig. 2]. This route was not merely convenient but symbolic since the new galleries were conceived as an extension to this richly ornamented Doric temple which had also been designed by Playfair. As Steell's massive statue of

Queen Victoria atop its northern portico proclaimed, the Institution was Crown property. It had been built in 1822 to provide headquarters for the Board of Manufactures, a uniquely Scottish government department whose origins lay in the Treaty of Union of 1707.

2. Royal Scottish Academy.
Copy of an engraving
from T. H. Shepherd's *Modern Athen..*

To relieve Scotland's all-pervasive poverty, a sum of money had been granted to the Board for the encouragement of manufactures. Since these tended to be rather humdrum household goods like textiles, the Board soon realised that the only means of making them more attractive for export lay in raising their standard of design. In 1760 it established a Drawing Academy in Edinburgh, one of the first schools of its kind in Britain. This bold innovative move was the first step in the Board's development into a body concerned with the promotion of art, and its Drawing Academy soon blossomed into a school with a broader curriculum in the fine arts. The school was to be accommodated in the new Institution building along with its teaching collections. These were housed in the attics because, in a grand gesture, the Institution was also to house Scotland's learned societies, whose distinguished members squeezed the students off the piano nobile.

The most prestigious of these tenants was the Royal Society of Edinburgh. Next in line came the Society of Antiquaries of Scotland. The most recently founded, the Institution for the Encouragement of the Fine Arts in Scotland, whose rather aristocratic membership achieved a Royal charter in 1827, made the most specialised demands on the architect. In addition to building up a permanent collection of works of art, the Institution held loan exhibitions of Old Masters and modern paintings which required a purpose-built modern gallery for their display. Although Playfair was only thirty-two years old, he had already demonstrated his capabilities at housing the city's intelligentsia after winning the competition to complete Robert Adam's design for Edinburgh University, where his uncle was one of its most celebrated professors. At the same time he proved that he could be trusted with public funds. Although the Board dug deeply into its own pocket for the new building, the real paymasters were in London and had little interest in Scottish pretensions. A tight budget was mandatory.

The Institution taught Playfair a number of lessons that were to stand him in good stead for its extension almost thirty years later. Although fashion decreed a Greek Temple solution, which was particularly appropriate for this open site, there was no way in which his clients' demands could be met with an internal logic that matched that of the exterior. Scientific attitudes to the display of pictures demanded that galleries should be top-lit. Playfair solved his problem by placing his galleries down the central axis, like the cella of a temple, around which the smaller and subsidiary rooms were fitted in with an eye more to convenience than creating a neat plan on paper. To avoid dim corners and ensure an expanse of evenly lit wall-surfaces, the two galleries were octagonal. The form of these galleries was so successful that it was to be duplicated in the National Gallery. In 1832, the burgeoning activities of the Institution's occupants required a further extension and the Board requested that the galleries should be extended to provide space for their own annual competitions of manufactured goods, which had reached a pitch of excellence under the direction of its brilliant Secretary, James Skene. By this time Playfair had entered his full artistic maturity which was to make him one of the greatest architects of his generation. As the trusted servant of the Board, he was able to win enough money, in the face of government parsimony, to give his building a more ornamental character, which is at its most eloquent in the deeply shadowed double lines of columns in the porticos, creating Piranesian effects in response to Edinburgh's uncertain climate. A programme of sculptural decoration reflected the Board's interest in ornamental design and culminated in Steell's statue of the youthful Queen, her gaze fixed prophetically northwards to Balmoral.

The foundations for this mass of masonry were to give Playfair especial problems. Since most of the site consisted of the 'travelled earth' excavated from New Town basements, a secure footing had only been achieved by sinking wooden piles in the Venetian manner deep into the ground. Although the full structural failure of this system did not occur until after Playfair's death, sufficient settlement took place to cause him considerable professional vexation and a determination to avoid this error the next time he built upon the Mound.

Even in its enlarged form the building failed to keep pace with the activities of its occupants. Although Playfair was in almost constant attendance to make adjustments and to shoe-horn yet more casts and bookcases into the limited space, there were certain problems that were beyond architectural solution. Since accommodation in the Institution was accepted as almost a stamp of seriousness and respectability, it was inevitable that all newly founded bodies concerned with the cultural life of the nation should attempt to nuzzle in under the Board's roof. The most important of these foundations was the Royal Scottish Academy, which was founded in 1826. Since the Institution contained the finest modern exhibition space in Scotland it was natural that the Academy should wish to hold their annual exhibitions there. At first the

Royal Institution for the Encouragement of the Fine Arts in Scotland and the Board were happy to hire their galleries to the Academy. However, as the occupants began to acquire their own permanent collections the Academy's annual usurpation caused considerable upheaval. In 1845 the Trustees of the Torrie Collection, recognising the advantages of the galleries, decided to deposit these important works of art with the Board, who were so much better equipped to display them than the original recipient, the College of Edinburgh. Since space within the building was so limited, the Academy's exhibitions could only be mounted at the expense of clearing the galleries of their valuable collections and placing them in store for the duration. As the Board were the guarantors for the safekeeping of the collections in their care, the Academy's exhibitions put them to a degree of risk which would have been unacceptable with goodwill on all sides.

In the 1840s, however, goodwill was at a premium on the Mound. As in most family quarrels no one had a monopoly of faults. The foundation of the Academy had been a secession from the Royal Institution, whom the artists held to be lukewarm in their support of living talent. As the disagreements mounted, the Institution's principal Academy-baiter, Alexander Maconochie of Meadowbank, accused the artists of chipping the Board's Doric columns as they delivered their pictures to the exhibitions. Playfair was called upon to design a contraption whose dual purpose was to protect his architecture and humiliate the junior body. The Board, who were perhaps too closely identified with the Institution and whose members were drawn from the nobility and the legal establishment, were particularly keen to shine as curators of other people's art after Lord Bute had offered the important collection at Luton House on temporary loan to Scotland, under a similar arrangement to that of the Torrie Trustees. For their part the Academy had an irritating tendency to print disagreeable correspondence in pamphlet form. Matters had come to a farcical head in 1844 with a row which erupted over the placing in the Academy's exhibition of a picture by the son of the Secretary of the Board, Sir Thomas Dick Lauder, whose hauteur of demeanour did little to promote harmony on the Mound. When the picture was purchased by the Royal Association for the Promotion of the Fine Arts, the Edinburgh Art Union and yet another of the newly founded bodies accommodated in the building, their patronage was taken for jobbery. Even Playfair, who as the Lauders' family friend and architect might have been expected to be partisan, took a dim view:

'The Association for the Fine Arts have bought young Lauder's miserable daub for thirty-five guineas – a complete prostitution of their power in my opinion and at the same time appearing to pass a censure on the artists of the Academy.'

This was the unedifying state of affairs that Sir John Shaw Lefevre had been sent to unravel. His credentials were impressive and lent great authority to his judgement. In 1832 he had been selected by the government to draw up the new boundaries for parliamentary constituencies required by the Reform Bill, which proved to be the foundation for a career including service on the Slave Compensation Commission, and an advisory role in the Amendment of the Poor Law Act and the foundation of South Australia. His investigation exposed the extent of official injustice to the Academy and recommended that it was essential for the artistic health of the nation that the Government should lend the artists a capital sum to enable them to build their own premises on the Mound. This would also provide space for the permanent display of those works of art already gathered on the Mound which Sir John had identified as the nucleus of a Scottish National Gallery.

The idea of a building on the Mound was far from new. In the early 19th century extensions to the original New Town had involved varying degrees of civil engineering to tame the city's geographical variety. To eyes attuned to the elegance of these new achievements in bridge-building, the gigantic heap of earth that had been the 18th century's solution to the problem of linking the Old and New Towns seemed unacceptably crude [Fig. 3]. Two opposing

3. View of the head of the Mound prior to the construction of the Free Church College and Wombwell's Menagerie

schools of thought developed. The first held that the Mound must be dignified by ornamental buildings. One of its most prominent campaigners, Alexander Trotter of Dreghorn, went so far as to obtain a plan from the Professor of Architecture in Venice for this important area of the city. Although on his return from his travels he had forgotten the Italian's name it did not prevent him from publishing the design in 1829. The other school held that the Mound was a sufficient error in its existing form and that nothing else must be allowed to disfigure further the natural beauties in the heart of the city. Not trusting the judgement of their fellow citizens, the latter school had obtained a series of Acts of Parliament to prevent any further interruption of the view from Princes Street.

Having obtained a foothold in 1822 on the Mound at the outset of his career with his Royal Institution building, the resolution of its town-planning problems was to occupy Playfair for the rest of his professional life. When the Academy's thoughts first turned to building they naturally asked Playfair, who was also a member, to prepare designs. The grandiose character of Playfair's design, comprising a pair of buildings with concave ends towards the Royal Institution and with the central carriageway passing under a triumphal arch on its ascent of the Mound, shows that it anticipated central government funding and was to accommodate rather more than the Academy. Such magnificent buildings would not only be costly in themselves and require several years to erect but, as his accompanying report made clear, a very great deal of preliminary negotiation would be necessary to put together the complex package that was essential to fund them and to acquire the land from its joint proprietors. The report also outlined local difficulties, which included the hazards of securing foundations on top of the railway tunnel which had just been forced through the Mound.

The necessary time for this gestation was a luxury that the Academy did not possess in 1845 since the Board's installation of the Torrie Collection in its Royal Institution Galleries effectively served the Academy with a notice to quit that building. With a growing sense of urgency they therefore wrote to instruct their architect to make out more detailed plans 'immediately'. Playfair replied from his sick-bed that this request was doubly tactless in that it showed that his employers were not only unaware of his severe in-disposition, but were also prepared to waive his professional advice that the proposals must proceed no further until the preliminary negotiations were completed. Since Playfair was so closely identified with the Board, the Academy's sworn enemy, it was perhaps inevitable that matters swiftly degenerated. In a spirit of bridge-building a deputation from the Academy called on their invalid architect but this only deepened the misunderstandings and Playfair sent in his resignation from the job on the grounds that:

'I may also add in my present weak state of health I feel very unequal to the anxiety and labour sure to attend the prosecution of this work, and am besides unwilling to encounter the strong conflict of opposite opinion and the violent discussions which I find is always met with in consideration of this business.'

Playfair seems to have been stung to the quick by the idea that the Academy were considering the erection of a cheap temporary structure on the Mound to provide an exhibition gallery until such time as his grand design could be realised. He was absolutely appalled that a body of artists could even con-template the addition of a further hut, which would be no better than Womb-well's Menagerie, to this sacred ground dedicated to the 'advancement of art'. He promptly despatched his resignation from the Academy:

'If therefore a temporary brick building is to be erected I am unwilling as an architect to be connected in any shape or form with such a deformity.'

The Academy attempted to mollify him and lamely explained that the raised voices on their part during the interview were out of consideration for his deafness, but Playfair refused to withdraw his joint resignation.

If his involvement with the 'building for the artists' had the effect of embroiling him in the domestic disputes which were being waged at the foot of the Mound, it bore more important fruit higher up the artificial hill.

The members of the newly-founded Free Church of Scotland nursed architectural ambitions and were keen to demonstrate their importance in Scottish life. In 1845 they were so fortunate as to acquire the prominent site at the head of the Mound. Anxious to shine, they held a competition for the design of a new building to house their college for the training of young ministers and invited Sir Charles Barry, the leading architect in Britain, to judge it. Conscious of the town-planning responsibilities which their building-site imposed, the results were deemed unworthy and Playfair was invited to design the new building. His involvement as architect arose because the Free Church initially intended to build an independent Assembly Hall on their portion of the Mound and it seemed natural to incorporate this in the western half of Playfair's splendid Doric buildings for the Academy.

His executed design went far beyond provision of the requisite accommodation for the fledgling College since its exterior was more for scenographic effect than an expression of the internal plan. Playfair identified a major axis up the Mound focusing on the tower of Tolbooth St John's Church, which was developed into a Durham Cathedral effect, and the College gatehouse was given twin towers to frame this most beautiful spire, whose elegant proportions were possibly ghosted by A. W. N. Pugin for its nominal architect, James Gillespie Graham. To read at a distance on the mile-long approach from Dundas Street, the height of the towers was exaggerated and they were given dramatically silhouetted terminals, their verticality emphasised with clusters of Beverley Minster buttresses. A third carefully placed tower enables the building to turn the corner most elegantly providing a further Picturesque grouping on the descent from the Old Town.

At the same time as he made this contribution to the permanent visual enrichment of Edinburgh, Playfair was also sowing the seeds for much personal pain. Having achieved a foreground and a background for the Mound through his two great buildings, there was always the possibility that an architect whose ideals for the profession were less exacting might be permitted to blot the middle distance. After the publication of Sir John Shaw Lefevre's report he had to endure the agony of a rival on this home ground. Playfair's resignation from the Academy left the way free for their Treasurer, the architect Thomas Hamilton, to present a design of his own in competition with Playfair [Fig. 4]. Although the former was sufficiently proud of his

Design for buildings on the Mound
to contain
the Royal Scottish Academy,
by Thomas Hamilton (1784-1858)

scheme to exhibit it in Paris and have the designs lithographed, it is perhaps easy to see why Playfair wrote 'I fear Hamilton who is full of intrigue and vulgar taste'. No less alarming was Barry's second appearance on the Mound as Treasury adviser on the proposed new buildings; he not only sent in a

proposal of his own [Fig. 5] but also suddenly reverted to the 'no building' line and suggested that Playfair might like to add a storey to his Institution building to contain a new exhibition room. Up to the point when he made this suggestion, Barry had been held in high esteem by Playfair as almost the only living architect who took his responsibilities seriously enough. Playfair returned a letter of absolutely chilling defiance with a copy to the Treasury.

It was extremely unusual for a British architect to regard such a large piece of topography as a private skittle-alley and Playfair's attitude to the Mound was a reflection of the exceptionally privileged position which he enjoyed in the 'Modern Athens' as the elected architect of its intelligentsia. On the continent his peers like Schinkel in Berlin and Von Klenze in Munich could count on direct royal patronage in their town-planning initiatives.

Although by 1850 there could be no doubt that Playfair was Scotland's greatest architect, it was not simply a matter of talent but rather of politics and social position too. After the death of his father, a Scottish architect who had been sufficiently successful to move to London, Playfair had been sent to Edinburgh so that his education could be supervised by his uncle, Professor John Playfair, a prominent Whig. In a natural progression his clients were to be very largely drawn from the city's intellectual and Whig circles. It was Playfair's good fortune architecturally that his artistic maturity coincided with the Whigs' emergence as a political force. His closest friend, whom he first met when they were schoolboys at the High School, was Andrew Rutherfurd. Their intimacy was such that Playfair adopted Andrew and his brother James for his own brothers. Bred for the law, Andrew embarked on a political career as Member of Parliament for Leith and through his great intellectual gifts rose to be Lord Advocate. Playfair's devotion to 'Madam Architecture' was so singleminded that he never married, so the Rutherfurds and their wives became his emotional mainstay. His professional progress was marred by a series of debilitating illnesses and, fully aware of his exceptional talents, the Rutherfurds and their mutual friends like Lord Cockburn were intensely protective of the architect.

5. Design for a new building on the Mound, c.1848. Watercolour, the design attributed to Sir Charles Barry (1795-1860)

As far as the Mound was concerned, Lord Rutherfurd with his 'uncon-ciliatory and somewhat haughty public demeanour' was all-powerful. A patron and promoter of art, the Lord Advocate was not only a member of the Board but a leading champion of the Royal Scottish Academy, and it was Lord Rutherfurd who, with Sir William Gibson Craig, had instigated Sir John Shaw Lefevre's investigation. As a prominent member of the Free Church, Lord Rutherfurd was undoubtedly influential in Playfair's appointment as its architect. Playfair was thus in an unusually advantageous position to in-fluence directly the developments on the Mound. At the time when his design was in rivalry with Hamilton's, for instance, Playfair suggested to Lord Rutherfurd that 'If the building could be erected and then handed over to the artists' a great deal of argument could be avoided, and this arrangement was eventually adopted. Cocooned from the world through devotion to his art and ill health, Playfair seems to have had little sense of gratitude for his privileged access to power and churlishly complained to Lord Rutherfurd: 'I sometimes think that having a friend in high office occasions one to be neglected while the stranger is attended to'. Playfair's exalted position was viewed less favourably by his fellow architects, who were deeply resentful that these negotiations were largely conducted 'behind closed doors'. The lack of any information to the press during these discussions fuelled very great ill feeling, particularly within the Royal Scottish Academy.

By 1849 the initial Lefevre proposal of making an interest-free loan to the Academy of £10,000 had run into difficulty. Since the building needs must cost more, the Academy would have had to borrow the difference, which would have saddled them with a crippling debt. Acting on his amended report of 5th May 1849, the Treasury resolved to erect a building on the Mound which would house both the Academy and a National Gallery.

THE DESIGN FOR THE NATIONAL GALLERY

It was to carry out this decision that on the 24th October 1849 Playfair, as 'the Board's architect', was instructed by the Board's new Secretary, the Hon. Bouverie Primrose, to prepare a design. Although Primrose, as the second son of the 4th Earl of Rosebery, was clearly well connected, it is possible that his appointment represented the replacement of a secretarial tradition of artistic amateurs like Skene and Lauder by a new breed of professional civil servants, since his early career had been spent in the Post Office. Primrose was to be a key figure in the erection of the National Gallery, which was to owe a great deal to his administrative abilities.

Playfair's position as architect was not an enviable one. He had resigned from the Academy which his design was to house, and between the Board and the Academy there was an atmosphere of mutual suspicion. Playfair's ability to work smoothly with these disunited elements owed much to his personal qualities. To a natural charm of manner he brought the tact of a lifetime's architectural experience. On several occasions during the building his social gifts were to enable him to resolve complicated disagreements smoothly and helped him to overlook his own quarrel with the Academy. The artists were given a private view of the design and Playfair 'invited the members if any improvement suggested itself to any of them, to communicate the same to him, promising to give all such hints his most careful consideration.'

In the later 1849 proposals there was a new note of realism. Although Playfair was summoned to London to explain his designs in person to the Chancellor of the Exchequer, 'whose close fist I shall try to relax', and won enough money to feel that he was 'on velvet instead of thorns', the Gallery was built to a tight budget and only sanctioned after hard estimates had been obtained. To ensure that funds were efficiently managed, £15,000 of the total cost was levied on the Board itself, leaving only £25,000 of the total of £40,000 to the mercy of a Parliamentary vote. In other circumstances this would have been a substantial sum, but since an unusual degree of civil engineering was required to shape the Mound and the site itself had to be purchased from the same budget, there was no extravagance or room for manoeuvre.

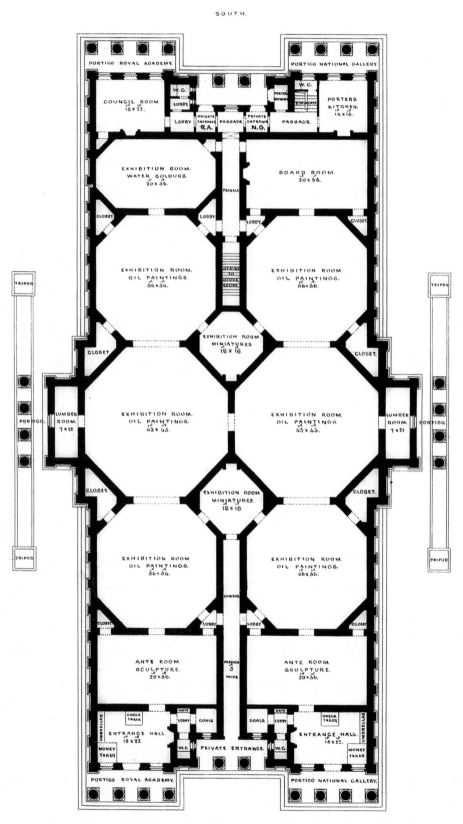

6. Preliminary plan with four columned porticos on the lateral facades

7. Preliminary sketch design for buildings on the Mound by William Henry Playfair

Playfair's design 'for the proposed buildings, being a finished perspective view, showing the position on the Mound, with a ground plan' was presented to the Board a week later on 31st October [Figs. 6 and 7]. The alacrity suggested by the Board's official record is misleading. There had been a great deal of discussion behind the closed doors of the Treasury and the first plan to show both the building and the roadway in its present form is dated 'August 1849'. It was characteristic of the very high regard in which Playfair was held that after his death his drawings were meticulously preserved in Edinburgh University Library, whereas the drawings of his architect contemporaries were regarded as mere business papers and have thus been scattered and lost.

Ironically, in spite of Playfair's devotion to the Mound, this disposition was not his, but Sir Charles Barry's. As the Treasury's professional adviser, Barry's final decision had been to reject both Playfair's and Hamilton's schemes for paired buildings on either side of the central carriageway. His reasoning was practical rather than aesthetic. If the two galleries which were to house the Royal Scottish Academy and the National Gallery were united under a single roof there would be only four, instead of eight, walls requiring expensive ornaments, and a single establishment could administer the whole. At the same time the roadway could have a more gentle gradient if it was taken up the western boundary of the Mound to return with a generous curve in front of the Free Church College.

Barry also stated that as the Board were to be responsible for the new building, their architect must design it. If the format, therefore, was pre-determined, Playfair was to be left with a free hand to develop the design, and the refinement of his ideas can be followed in the drawings which he produced in the ensuing months. There were two problems to be solved. The first was to create a set of galleries lit from above as scientific attitudes to the display of pictures demanded.

The second was essentially a town-planning problem, in that the building had to be blended into its naturally beautiful setting in such a way that it could not detract from the rugged grandeur of the Castle rock and, if possible, it must enhance the scene [Fig. 7]. Unusually the site was not only visible from every direction, but also from above, looking down from the Old Town, and from below, when glimpsed from Princes Street Gardens. Playfair came to see his Gallery as being like the hub of a wheel, the centre-point of the great cyclorama of North Edinburgh which embraces the Firth of Forth and, on a clear day, the mountains of the Highlands. The Gallery responds to these demands in a design which boxes the compass, closing all the many sight-lines with interesting Picturesque effects. To an unusual extent the building's two functions of interior practicality and external effect are mutually exclusive because, since the galleries are top-lit, the long facades which are unbroken by windows do not need to reflect the interior disposition.

The key to the plan [Fig. 8] consists of the two parallel galleries which provided identical accommodation for the annual exhibitions of the Royal Scottish Academy to the east and the new National Gallery to the west. In the light of the recent history of the Mound it is possible to see Playfair distributing the available space with scrupulous fairness like an exasperated parent dividing a limited quantity of sweets between two quarrelling children. Each gallery consisted of three octagons, and this arrangement reflected the final arrangement of the Royal Institution exhibition rooms. However, by breaking outwards the centre of the external side walls of the building, Playfair was able to make the central compartments into pure octagons which can be inscribed within a square as against the irregular octagon, inscribed within a rectangle, of the Royal Institution's central room. In terms of traditional Scottish architecture these two great octagons have parish church dimensions and they were thus able to accommodate the largest canvases. In an ingenious piece of 'honey-comb' planning the doubling-up of the two galleries permitted the formation of a pair of smaller octagons, one for each occupant, in the dead spaces formed by the cut-away corners. As Playfair's section shows [Fig. 9], each cell varies in height and the *Building Chronicle* explains that this arose from a desire to match their different areas of wall surface to the amount of light entering from above so that the suite is evenly lit. A series of jib doors between the paired galleries enabled them to function in tandem when required.

In the Royal Institution the octagons had been conceived as individual rooms, although they could be thrown together if required by opening the large double doors which separated them and which, ingeniously, disappeared into slots cut into the party walls. In the National Gallery, by contrast, the octagons were interlinked by deep 'railway-tunnel' arches whose depth arose from the necessity for strong construction and which allowed for additional hanging space on the flanks. Although these arches bear a resemblance to those in other 19th-century galleries such as Sir John Soane's celebrated Dulwich Gallery, their effect is different. Whereas at Dulwich it looks as though the Gallery has been built up by the repetition of small units, in Edinburgh the dynamic perspective of the picture-hung tunnel-arches means that the eye reads the octagons as a single long gallery which has been moulded into this complicated shape for dramatic effect.

8. Plan of the National Gallery, 1852

9. Composite sections and plan of the mezzanine floor at the south en

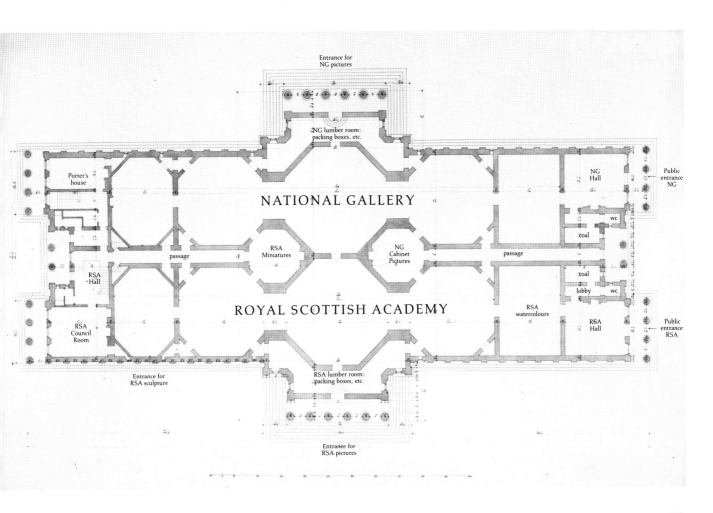

Entrance for
NG pictures

NG lumber room:
packing boxes, etc.

Porter's
house

NG
Hall

Public
entrance
NG

NATIONAL GALLERY

wc

coal

RSA
Miniatures

NG
Cabinet
Pictures

passage

passage

RSA
Hall

coal

lobby

wc

ROYAL SCOTTISH ACADEMY

RSA
watercolours

RSA
Hall

Public
entrance
RSA

RSA
Council
Room

Entrance for
RSA sculpture

RSA lumber room:
packing boxes, etc.

Entrance for
RSA pictures

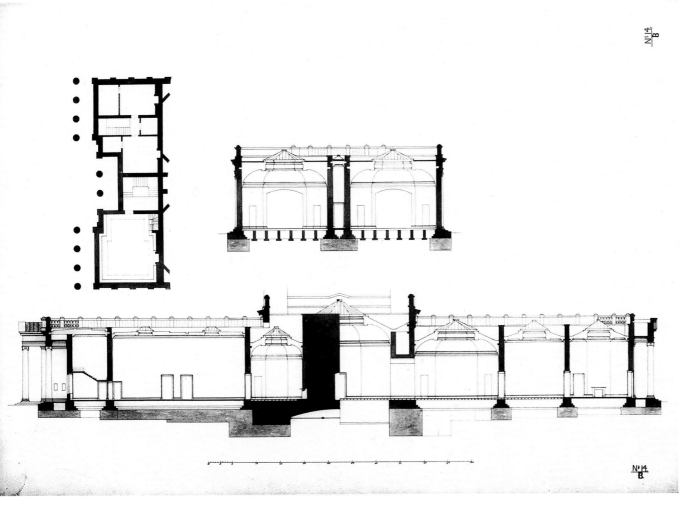

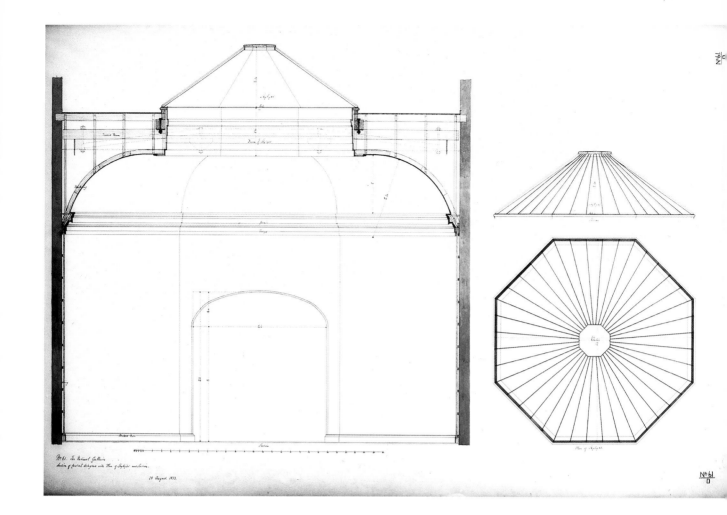

10. Section through a central octagon showing rooflight and construction

Although the octagons were given matching handsomely profiled cornices and surbases, and no architect ever took more care in designing his profiles than Playfair, they are pared of all extraneous ornament [Fig. 10]. The deep coves above the cornices, whose function is to bounce the light from the overhead cupolas onto the wall-faces, are absolutely plain. This rationalism of design was so extreme that the wall-surfaces consisted of plain painted vertical planking which, as seen in old photographs, seems almost shocking to modern eyes attuned to damask. This arrangement repeated the design of the Royal Institution galleries and allowed for the direct fixing of the largest canvases. One area of advance on the earlier galleries lay in the heating system. The National Gallery was heated by hot air from grilles in the floor rather than by open fires, which were considered dangerous, although fireplaces were provided in the two small central octagons. Even in the Royal Institution the fireplaces in the Board's exhibition rooms had been suppressed in order to release more picture-hanging space. A central spinal corridor allowed access to the heating chamber and for the supply of coals to fuel the fireplaces in the central octagon.

At either end of the central tri-partite galleries, their occupants were provided with another exhibition room. In execution the northern of these was united to the central compartments by repeated railway-tunnel arches which upset the balance of the design. On the north front, nearest the parent building, each occupant had their individual but identical entrance halls opening from the pair of porticos. It was only at the south end of the plan that strict symmetry was departed from to provide the Academy with its Council Room, with windows in the portico, and a top-lit library above. The equivalent compartment on the western side provided a house for a resident custodian. In this ingenious plan there is not a single useless door nor a wasted space. The large portico doors to the east and west open directly into the largest octagons, allowing easy access for pictures through conveniently situated unpacking or 'lumber rooms'. One modification suggested by the Academy was the provision of large external doors in the east facade to service the exhibition room, which they had decided to devote to sculpture and which was thus able to cope with the largest sculptural works.

A preliminary plan which may be that which Playfair presented to the Board on the 31st October shows that the interior underwent only minor modification. This rational interior has been married to an exterior which is romantically Picturesque and which was to pass through several stages before it reached its executed solution. The dual occupancy is expressed by the paired porticos on the north and south fronts. Further screens of columns across the central service doors create a richly modelled effect. It is the major east and west facades, however, which dominate the townscape. The side walls had necessarily to break outwards in the centre to accommodate the larger central

1. Perspective study of preliminary design with a Doric order which has been kept as low as possible to avoid interfering with the view of the Castle from East Princes Street

2 (below). Edinburgh Castle and the National Gallery. Photographer unknown

octagons, and the preliminary plan shows that Playfair initially intended to mark these entrances by small four-columned porticos identical with the pairs on the north and south fronts. These would have been too small in relation to the great length of these facades and by the time of the first perspective they had been increased to six columns, although they supported the same entablature. This drawing shows an unsatisfactory suggestion for screening the rooflight with a false roof, which simply disappeared in the middle of the building [Fig. 11].

Like all the early schemes, this sketch displays a Doric order, reflecting the Royal Institution. Although this was necessarily a prerequisite for the elaborate early schemes with paired buildings to give continuity, the asymmetry of Barry's arrangement meant that it became logical for Playfair to develop a deliberate contrast between his buildings for Picturesque effect. His choice of the Ionic order bowed to a traditional idea that it was particularly appropriate for artists but it also suited the more elevated structure. Although Playfair's early perspective made it look as though the two buildings were to be on the same level, the slope of the Mound necessarily entailed that the National Gallery had to stand on a terrace elevated above the Royal Institution. Since the Ionic order is more attenuated than the Doric, the height of the building began to increase.

There were practical considerations too. The new form of the Mound which encircled the National Gallery on its ascent must have given rise to a real concern that the building would have a sunken effect, as though concealed in a bunker. The two most important sight-lines were from the open roadway as it descended from the Bank of Scotland and from the gate of his Free Church College [Fig. 12]. To solve this problem Playfair decided to raise the height of the central section of the building which had already broken forward laterally beyond its rectangular confines. The wall-head is sufficiently high to prevent a pedestrian on the Mound being able to peer into its central well. These high attics, like the very un-Greek balustrades which run round the outer walls, serve the practical function of concealing the skylights (although they cannot compete against their hideous 20th-century replacements). It is immediately obvious on the roof of the central section that their height has been exaggerated beyond all practical need to conceal the rooflights, since the attic walls tower above the spectator as though in a high-security prison. There were additional bonuses for the side views from Princes Street since the increased height of the lateral porticos meant that they could play an appropriate role in the townscape. In his final design Playfair intended to exaggerate this effect still further by the addition of Corinthian terminals [Fig. 13] which seem to owe more to King's College Chapel in Cambridge, one of Playfair's favourite buildings, than to Hellenistic inspiration.

Although Playfair is conventionally considered to be a Greek Revival architect it is clear that this design is *sui generis* and arose as a direct response to the needs of the occupants and more importantly the site. Playfair's architectural education, unlike that of C. R. Cockerell, with whom he collaborated on the National Monument on Calton Hill, had not embraced any voyages of architectural discovery and he seems to have had little interest in the academic quotation of earlier architectural designs which all too often are thought to be especially suitable for art galleries. The departures from the more doctrinaire aspects of the Greek Revival are notable. These include the use of a giant and a minor order; the raising of the central section four steps above the flanks for external effect, although the galleries are actually on the same level, and the fact that the pilasters that pace out the side walls do not coincide with the internal wall divisions.

13. Elevation of central section showing proposed Corinthian terminal

14. Full-size design for the Ionic volutes

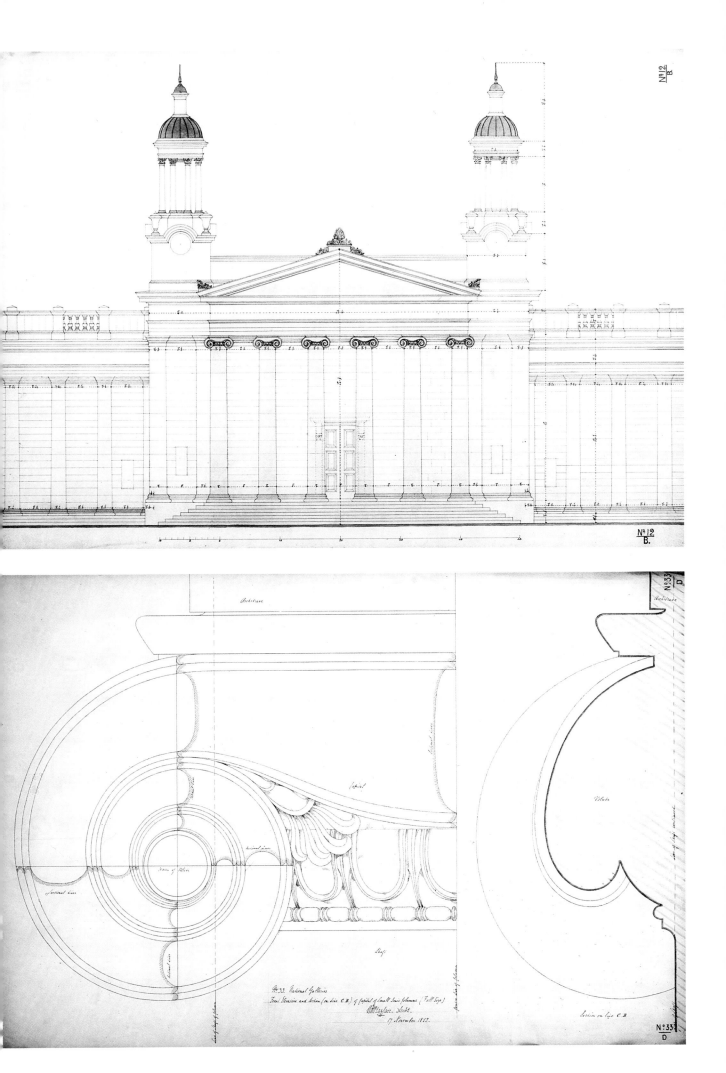

Playfair's version of the Ionic order appears to be one which satisfied personal aesthetic feelings instead of quoting from an antique prototype, and it would have been inconceivable to him that such details, on which the beauty of the building depended, should not be most carefully designed by the architect, as his meticulous full-size drawings demonstrate [Fig. 14]. The *Building Chronicle*'s account of the building stated:

'Throughout the structure a system of curved surfaces has been resorted to, apparently based on the results of Mr Penrose's investigations on the Parthenon; in which, as our readers will remember no literal straight line could be found.'

In spite of their difference in style both the National Gallery and the Free Church College show an architect able to sculpt the silhouettes of his buildings for purely scenographic effect and thus fit them for their position in the very heart of one of Europe's most beautiful cities. The National Gallery's lack of ornament must, in part, have been the result of the financial stringency imposed by the Treasury, which was certainly responsible for the excision of the Corinthian terminals and a Hollywoodesque flight of steps, as wide as the eastern portico, which was to descend into Princes Street Gardens.

However, the studied simplicity must also reflect a personal aesthetic which refined the design through the editing away of all extraneous features. The vases which were to have been placed over each die on the balustrade were an early casualty but the same process is noticeable on more subtle details, such as the omission of the consoles to the doorways which are shown on the early drawings. When the entablature was placed on the great western portico and the citizens of Edinburgh could appreciate fully the austerity of their new building, Playfair wrote revealingly to Lord Rutherfurd:

'I feel sure that the architecture of this building will be too simple and pure to captivate the multitude, but I am certain I follow the right path in what I am doing and so am content.'

It could be argued that in the design of the National Gallery Playfair, who was then fifty-nine years old and in indifferent health, was conscious that this might be his final work and was seeking to leave a testament. The astringency of his vision is more apparent through an invidious comparison with the florid Venetian High Renaissance headquarters of the Life Association of Scotland at 82 Princes Street, which was Barry's unexpected contribution to the Moundscape in 1855 [Fig. 15]. However, that Playfair was not altogether happy with the absence of ornament is suggested by the knowledge that, through Lord Cockburn, Playfair pressed the Academy to agitate for sculpture in the east and west pediments.

BUILDING THE NATIONAL GALLERY

The realisation of this design was to take ten years. The Board's first task was the acquisition of the site. The Free Church gladly parted with the western sector of the Mound for £3,000. They had a vested interest in Playfair's improvements since they would show their building off to greater advantage. The eastern section of the site and the area occupied by the Gallery itself belonged to the City of Edinburgh. As leading supporters of the Academy the Town Council parted with it magnanimously at the nominal sum of £1,000. This generosity was not purely selfless since strings were attached to the sale and it gave them an interest in the building which helped to ensure that the promise to the Academy was honoured.

15. View of the Royal Institution,
c.1858.
Photograph by W. D. Clarke
(died 1873)

The levelling of the site to form the terrace on which the Gallery sits and to shape the carriageway necessitated a large expenditure in itself. The Treasury were so intent on speed of execution that Playfair was permitted to begin work before his contract drawings were completed. The excavated earth was used for improvements to Princes Street Gardens. A pessimism engendered by five years of abortive schemes was reflected in the preface to this instruction which declared that the levelling would be a useful exercise 'even supposing the new buildings were not erected.' The existing services which crossed the Mound presented additional difficulties. These comprised the main water-pipe to the New Town and the sewer from the Old Town. The mains-pipe was re-routed through a new channel to the east of the site since there was a real fear that the great pressure of the water could sweep the buildings away in the event of an accident. The sewer was mistakenly seen as a lesser problem. These changes involved the Board in much preliminary legal wrangling and a judicial survey of the entire site was drawn up to prevent later disputes. In all these endeavours Playfair benefited from the counsel of James Jardine, the civil engineer.

On the advice of Lord Cockburn, who had laboured for many years in the cause of the Academy and who had been given a seat on the Board, it was felt that it would be essential to obtain a new Act of Parliament for the erection of the building and the re-routing of the carriageway in case the development was challenged under the existing legislation. For political reasons more relevant to London than Edinburgh, however, the name of the Academy was withheld from the Act's wording, which fuelled real fears that their interests were being neglected. Playfair produced the completed working drawings in June 1850, which enabled the building work to be put out to tender. The drawings had been originally promised for January but Playfair stated that the delay had resulted from his summons to London to explain his design to the Treasury. Secretary Primrose was clearly concerned to have the detailed plans approved by the Treasury so that they were fully aware of their commitments on the Mound.

These negotiations acquired a new urgency when the Board found its hand forced in the matter of the foundation ceremony. The Lord Provost of Edinburgh, Sir William Johnstone, had issued a personal invitation to Prince Albert during his presentation in London. The Prince's willingness to officiate was reported to the Board on the 19th June, together with the news that the Royal family would break their long journey to Balmoral at Holyrood in August. This left only a few weeks to finalise plans for the ceremony and also posed a certain embarrassment since the foundations had not even been cut. News of the Royal presence did much to expedite the progress of the legislation, since the Queen could hardly give her approval to a building whose cost had yet to be voted through Parliament.

Playfair's health had been precarious for many years and when he was invited by the Board to supervise the arrangements he replied that 'he scarcely felt his strength equal to the hurry and responsibility of this undertaking'. It was therefore his Clerk of Works, James Pitbladdo, who accompanied the working drawings to London, where they were presented to Parliament. The arrangements for the ceremony were delegated to Robert Matheson, architect of the Office of Works, who had thrown himself into the task of renovating the derelict Holyrood for the reception of the Queen with characteristic gusto. The excitement of the event and speed of execution seem to have led to a loss of financial control, and there was much social jockeying for position. The Board were fully alive to their responsibilities as reformers of national taste and the trowel which the Prince was to use in the ceremony and retain as a souvenir, 'according to custom', was designed by Alexander Christie, Manager of the Board's School. Like everything else it exceeded its estimates and if this piece of 'massive silver-gilt' emblazoned with the Arms of Scotland and the Board is ever traced, it will be one of the most important pieces of documented Scottish silver in existence and the touch-stone of the Board's taste.

As a result of the most careful preparations and rehearsal the ceremony was outstandingly successful. The real hero of the day was Playfair himself because during the afternoon the Queen had inspected his newly completed masterpiece, Donaldson's Hospital. Lord Cockburn described these events in a letter to a mutual friend:

'Think of Pluffy's felicity yesterday. At one o'clock Albert laid the foundation of his galleries, and at 4 the Queen went over his Hospital, *speaking much to the architect himself* and admiring everything. It was his great day and delighted, modest and amiable he was – in spite of all the laughter and parodies that I could exhaust myself in pouring out on him. The foundation stone is a great event. It greatly adorns Edinburgh and saves it from a fatal change which nothing but an ornamental appropriation of the ground could have avoided.'

Playfair's own response is revealing of his attitude to architecture:

'I am like to laugh at the smiles frequently bestowed on me since the Queen and the Prince spoke to me at the Hospital by people who would have hardly acknowledged the architect before. Fools! Don't they see it is the architecture that is noticed and not the man. If the Queen ever were to confer any mark of distinction on me it should surely be when the National Gallery shall be finished and found worthy which with God's aid it may be.'

The total cost of the morning's activities amounted to £859 8s. 10d. Primrose expected to be reimbursed for this substantial sum directly by the Treasury, so the news that it must be paid out of the National Gallery's Building Fund must have been a shock.

The rearrangement of the services on the Mound must have seemed a relatively simple matter when compared with the calculations necessary for the foundations. Not only was Playfair aware of the onset of failure in the Royal Institution's system of wooden piles, but there was the added difficulty of building over the railway.

When the tunnel was first projected in 1837 there had been an understandable anxiety for the safety of the Royal Institution's foundations and in his report Playfair stated that it was:

'I think difficult to imagine any formation of ground, or any combination of circumstances more unfavourable to the production of a good and stable foundation for a building.'

Playfair's solution was to centre his building over the tunnel to ensure that the weight was evenly distributed [Fig. 16]. To minimise direct pressure on the tunnel linings the great central section of the Gallery is actually carried on a shallow bridge formed from a series of stone arches, strengthened with

16. Section through the foundations of the central section showing the method of bridging the tunnel and the supporting girders

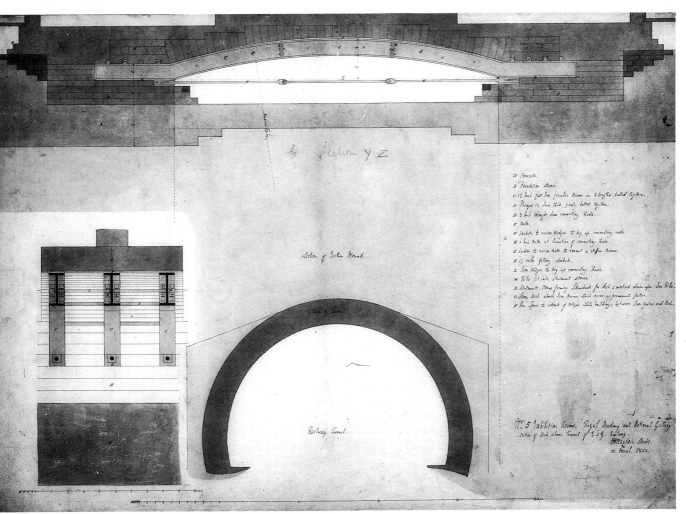

iron beams arranged in triplets under each wall so that the stresses are relayed sideways from the tunnel itself. The girders used to strengthen the foundations were identical in their construction to the system Playfair had adopted for the support of Steell's massive statue of Queen Victoria over the north portico of the Royal Institution, whose weight proved far greater than he had anticipated. The foundations rest on a matrix of concrete thickening towards the centre where the pressure was greatest. Playfair relished the solution to this kind of technical problem, as a letter of 1852 shows:

'I have this day struck the centre of the first arch across the Edinburgh and Glasgow Railway Tunnel which will carry some of the walls of the National Gallery. I had prepared for it sinking 2 inches in the keystone and it has subsided only 1 inch and 5/8ths. This appears to me to be a good work of construction when it is recollected that the arch is 40 foot in span and rises only 3 feet and the keystones only 2 feet in depth. A segment of a semi-circle as this is a segment of a circle 140 foot in diameter so small a sinking in a 2 foot keystone on a forty foot segment of so large an arch is very satisfactory.'

Work of this precision depended on the skills of the best available tradesmen. Characteristically, Playfair had won the right not to have to employ the contractors who sent in the lowest tenders, and the stonework was entrusted to David Lind, who was the most expensive. Playfair justified the extra cost on the grounds that Lind was the tenant of the Binny Quarry, whose honey-coloured stone had been selected, and he would therefore be able to maintain a steady flow of excellent masonry. Lind's stonework is of outstanding quality and fully justified Playfair's confidence. On close inspection it is apparent that the severity has been relieved by a variety of textures. Although the shafts of the capitals and pilasters have been polished to an exceptionally smooth surface, the wall-faces have been dressed with chisel marks to provide a lively contrast. Sadly, the sharpness of many of the details which enabled contemporaries to compare this sandstone to marble has been lost through abrasive cleaning and the deleterious effects of 'Auld Reekie's' atmosphere.

Struck by the immense foundations, the *Building Chronicle* exclaimed in wonderment that 'something like £5,000 has been buried underground.' The site exerted a great fascination on the curious and the idle. Although the iron railings were erected rapidly on the Mound, the carpenters, Goodall and Sanderson, were asked to erect a wooden palisade around the site which was 'found absolutely necessary to protect the iron railing which ran the risk of being thrown down or broken by the number of people pressing upon it and looking over to see the work going on in the enclosed ground below.' The paling remained a prominent feature of the centre of Edinburgh for several years and its appearance was captured in a photograph by Thomas Keith [Fig. 17].

As the confusion of the huge building-site departed and the bones of the design began to be appreciable, there was general satisfaction in the new amenity value of the Mound, which previously had been a sea of Macadamised mud. As early as August 1851 Playfair could report to James Rutherfurd:

'I cannot resist the pleasure of telling you that after more than a year's troublesome and incessant labour I have at length levelled and cleared the Ground so as to be able to commence the National Gallery. I have transferred the road across the Mound from the eastern to the western side and have by removing many thousand cubic yards of earth brought the general surface to a dead level and the contractor begins tomorrow, God Willing, to dig out the trenches for the concrete and the foundations. The West Road up which people now pass, exhibits a very agreeable view of the Western Gardens and

7. The National Gallery
nearing completion.
Photograph by Dr Thomas Keith
(1827-95)

of the Castle Rock. The Free Church College appears to rise out of a green bank and the road is so easy that a cab can be trotted up without difficulty. The Great Iron Pipe of the Crawley Spring and its stone tunnel in which it reposed has been moved from the centre to the side of the Mound, to make way for the foundations of the National Gallery and no accident has occurred.'

Characteristically, Playfair pressed for the early planting of trees and shrubs on the Free Church ground near Ramsay Lodge to landscape the Mound. His interest in blending his buildings into their settings through the softening effect of natural vegetation had received an early stimulus during his initial training with William Stark, the short-lived Scottish architect whose report on the Calton Hill development preferred crags and trees to regularity and profit.

Encouraged by the success of these labours, Playfair presented his bill for professional services, which amounted to £798. It was only now that Playfair asked to be remunerated for the series of abortive designs which had commenced with the 1845 scheme for the Royal Scottish Academy. His account listed four separate projects before the executed design and they can all be identified among his drawings in Edinburgh University Library. The most surprising item was the total of eighty-seven days spent in London on three different occasions to explain his designs. His letter ended 'But not being a wealthy man I cannot without difficulty and inconvenience wait longer.' His claim was settled immediately.

His professional skills were soon put to the test by the bankruptcy of the contractors for the carpentry, Goodall and Sanderson. Since the complexities of the Gallery rooflights involved a considerable quantity of ironwork they had subcontracted this part of the work and 'bargained with a foundry to execute it at an absurdly low rate.' The new contractor, Turnbull, was unwilling to perform the work for the same sum and so a new contract for the ironwork was offered to Miller and Co., who had successfully carried out the ironwork of the foundations. This setback added to the total expenditure and a tiresome dispute about Goodall and Sanderson's stockpile of timber on the Mound already delivered to the site occupied much valuable time.

This problem, however, was trivial in comparison to the news which was broken to the Board on 31st October 1853 that Playfair had been stricken by serious illness. He appears to have suffered a stroke which left him partially paralysed. Its immediate effects were sufficiently alarming for the Rutherfurds to believe it was the final illness. On the 23rd of that month Lord Rutherfurd had written that he was:

'Deeply grieved for poor Playfair, of whom I also heard from Edinburgh. He is very bad, though I have long suspected such an end – but he should have been permitted to be *finished* the works he had in hand.'

Since his designs had been completed, Secretary Primrose felt confident that with the assistance of 'Mr James Hamilton, Mr Playfair's Principal Clerk and with Mr Pitbladdo, the clerk of works, he had satisfied himself that the works could be carried on properly' until the architect was restored to health. By April of 1853 the walls of the western portico had risen to the level of the entablature. The Ionic capitals were modelled for the masons by the plasterer, Annan, and Playfair had the satisfaction of knowing that 'My building is beginning to win golden opinions from the Public who have been very slow to move.' Lord Cockburn's death in April 1854 was a further indication that the brilliant generation of 'Modern Athenians', to which Playfair himself belonged, was beginning to disintegrate.

The building was by now sufficiently advanced to permit the installation of Hadden's hot air system. As the galleries began to take shape, experiments were made to test the system of top-lighting. Sir John Watson Gordon was inspired to suggest an alteration which he felt would improve the display of sculpture. After a demonstration involving a bust, it was found that Sir John's system in a frontal view brought some benefit, but since it left the back in obscurity his idea was abandoned, which fully vindicated Playfair's methods. These advances within, however, were offset by external problems when it was discovered that the main sewer was in a precarious condition. To apportion responsibility for its repair the Board had to resort to law.

THE FIRST EXHIBITION

On the 14th August 1854 the Royal Scottish Academy petitioned the Board for permission to hold their 1855 exhibition in the eastern galleries, which were nearing completion. They were confident that the novelty value of the new setting would bring forth an exceptional crop of pictures but their real anxiety was to force the Board to acknowledge the precise terms under which the Academy would occupy their side of the building. The sudden death of Lord Rutherfurd deprived the Academy of one of its most important champions and when this event was given by the Board as a reason for postponing any decision it looked like prevarication, and the Academy's Secretary, D. O. Hill, wrote to insist that they were put in occupation 'with as little delay as possible'. In their indignation, as so often before, the correspondence was set in print. The architect reported that the eastern side would be ready for the 1855 exhibition, whose usual starting date was cheerfully delayed to allow time for fitting up the apartments. At the Board's meeting to decide the regulations for the management of the new building Sir William Gibson Craig, as a member of the Board, presented a proposal for the distribution of the accommodation. Since he had been Lord of the Treasury when the design was agreed, his suggested arrangements were identical to the original specification which must have been issued to Playfair. A sinister note was struck, however, in the stipulation that the Academy would hold exclusive rights to their galleries on the eastern side only during their annual exhibition and that the Board reserved the right to use them for other purposes connected with the promotion of art at the Treasury's pleasure. After a certain amount of wrangling, in which the Academy had to remind the Board of the terms under which the city had sold the site, the Gibson Craig proposals were unanimously accepted.

The Academy's immediate priority was to finish the galleries in time for the exhibition and these fears for the future could be set on one side. Since the contractor, Turnbull, was not required to finish them before October 1855, a great deal had to be done at the last minute, which led him to claim compensation subsequently. It is clear that the opening was regarded as a makeshift affair. The linings were given only two coats of paint by Ballantine and Allan in a colour selected by the President. Impressed by the efficiency of the gas lighting used at the Scottish Exhibition of Arts and Manufactures in Glasgow, the Academy carried out similar experiments on the Mound. If the results should prove successful, the Board agreed to pay the final bill but if they were deemed unsuitable, the Academy would have both to pay up and have them removed. All these preparations were completed for the Academy's first exhibition in its new home, which opened on 5th April 1855 with a splendid reception. The help extended by Playfair's clerk of works, James Pitbladdo, was acknowledged by the presentation of an inscribed watch from the Academy.

Behind this surface glitter, however, the Building Committee had run into trouble. As the Board took stock a bleak picture emerged from the accounts. The total sum provided for the erection of the Gallery up to the 7th March 1855 had been £40,669, while £40,478 had been disbursed. All works were stopped immediately. Since no one knew when building would be recommenced, the precaution was taken of spending the balance of £191 on the painting of the linings of the western half, which the architect deemed essential for their preservation. The future of the building rested in Primrose's hands and the report which he drew up for the Treasury.

Primrose was at pains to show that he had been conscious of 'exercising a sound and vigilant check on the expenditure' and that no blame could be attached to the Board since the extra costs arose through 'the peculiar nature of the site'. The architect's struggles against the combined forces of the railway tunnel, the mass of earth, the water main and the sewer were dramatically reported. Reminding their Lordships that the plans had been 'submitted to and approved by the Treasury' Primrose went on to state that the designs:

'While beautiful in conception and in effect, are characterised by the greatest simplicity and severest taste, and no expense has been incurred in decoration or ornament internally or externally that could be avoided.'

Once the Gallery was finished and the two buildings were run in parallel they would form 'An Institution for the promotion of art unrivalled in the kingdom.' The recent opening of the eastern side had received:

'The most unqualified approbation of the Academy, who if required will certify to your Lordships their entire approbation of the arrangement and distribution of light in the galleries. They have been received with the greatest admiration by the public and the strongest feeling is entertained that the beautiful Building so ornamental to the city, should be completed without delay.'

It must have given Primrose satisfaction to read the Treasury's reply at the Board's meeting of 21st May which showed how effectively his eloquence had moved the stony hearts of their Lordships, although their reply was prefaced by the remark that they 'had learned with much regret that the very large and liberal grant had fallen so far short.' The extra £10,000 which had been estimated as the necessary sum for completion was granted but there was a sting in the tail, in so far as the Treasury would only sanction £5,000, which had to be matched by the Board. The Board's finances had been efficiently managed, however, and their initial £15,000 had been raised through advantageous selling of stock on the advice of Mr Mitchell Innes and the Royal Bank. Primrose's only error of judgement in his report was to linger in a little too much detail on the expense of the foundation ceremony, which brought down the riposte that the Treasury regretted 'that so very large a sum as £861 of Public money, had been expended in the mere ceremony of laying the foundation stone of the Building.'

The way was now clear to finishing the buildings, although the matching of the sums was an effective Treasury device to ensure financial stringency. The principal remaining problem was the sewer. It was an urgent one for the Gallery because until it was repaired the drains could not be connected, which left the foundations vulnerable to flood damage. In heavy rain a large volume of water was thrown off the Mound and had to be carried off in pails by the workmen before it seeped into the foundations. The Board were eventually found liable for £1,132 as against the city's £19 8s. 1d., and it was held that the construction of the foundations had damaged the sewer. Of rather more architectural moment was the design of the eastern footpath and the stairway connecting it to the Mound. Since this directly involved the City as proprietors of the adjoining ground, much thought was given to the necessary security arrangements. It was eventually agreed that the design should take in an extra strip of city land to make it 'wider and straighter', and to close the steps experimentally at night with gates whose keys would be entrusted to the gardener.

In the haste of fitting up the eastern side, the gas-fitters, Haldane and Rae, so misunderstood their instructions from the Royal Scottish Academy that they supplied fittings throughout the building. Owing to this mistake the 'Board was involved in expenditure which they might have hesitated to undertake had they been applied to at the time'. For his part Haldane was 'entangled in an embarrassment' and 'due to the size and peculiar shape of the Apartments of the National Gallery' there was little hope of being able to re-sell the fittings or recover the cost of the moulds. The architect's tactful solution was to suggest a reduction of $7\frac{1}{2}\%$ on the bill.

The first opening of the National Gallery side happened by accident rather than design. The Manager of the Board's School, Alexander Christie, who was a leading light in the Art Manufacturers Association, had applied to the Board for support and permission to hold their proposed exhibition in the east galleries immediately prior to the next Royal Scottish Academy exhibition. Since the aims of the Association were attuned to those of the Board, permission was granted although some suggestions for improvement in the Association's management were requested. Their success in attracting exhibits was so great that permission to use the west galleries, which 'stood perfectly empty', was requested. This was granted and so, ironically, the National Gallery side, which was to be dedicated to Fine Art, opened with an exhibition of Decorative Art.

Primrose was under great pressure within Scotland to have the National Gallery opened. His own staff at the Board petitioned him about the expected new posts that would arise. Both Christie and W. B. Johnstone of the Royal Scottish Academy applied for the job of curator. The Society of Antiquaries, who in the complicated game of musical chairs on the Mound had been promised the Royal Institution galleries, when vacated, for their Museum, were particularly anxious to see the National Gallery established. Primrose's own uncertainty about the building's future led him to open negotiations with the Office of Works to see if they might take on their maintenance.

THE DEATH OF PLAYFAIR AND FURTHER DIFFICULTIES

Tragically, the slow pace of Victorian bureaucracy meant that Playfair did not live to see the opening of the completed National Gallery, and the Board's meeting on 30th March opened with the melancholy news of his death. A long encomium was entered in the minutes:

'The Board desires to record in the Minutes its extreme regret for the loss the Public has sustained by the death of Mr Playfair and its high appreciation of his Architectural works, which are not only most ornamental to the City of Edinburgh but cannot fail to have a favourable influence on National Taste. The Board would particularly refer to its two buildings constructed by him – The Royal Institution and The National Gallery – edifices, in which he had to contend with difficulties of no small magnitude and which are admirably adapted to the purposes for which they were intended, and which will transmit his name as the first of the Classic school of Scottish Architects. In recording the loss it has sustained, the Board cannot refrain from adding to the regret it feels that Mr Playfair should not have lived to see the completion of his National Galleries.'

There could surely be no more moving tribute to Playfair's architecture than the Board's belief that it had served a didactic purpose in their artistic programme. His assistant, James Hamilton, was appointed to complete the galleries.

During their 1857 exhibition the Academy had been permitted the use of the National Gallery side for an evening reception. As the company circulated round the building, it soon became obvious to all that while the Royal Scottish Academy was brilliantly lit, the National Gallery was plunged in gloom. Since they had identical gas-fittings the fault must lie elsewhere. It was eventually discovered that through the joint occupation of the building the gas had come to be supplied by different companies who maintained different pressures. This absurdity was rapidly solved when the Edinburgh Gas Company was asked to supply both sides.

The final details of finishing the building fell to Hamilton. These largely consisted of ironing out last-minute snags. His only opportunity for original design came with the vases at the foot of the Mound steps, although even this was subject to Steell's approval, and the railing along the pathway, which he cribbed from Schinkel's published designs. The shallowness of the steps, however, was held to be dangerous, as was the check for the gate in the centre of the pathway. Hamilton put up a vigorous defence of his master:

'I need not remind the Board with what attentive and scrupulous solicitude the late Mr Playfair ever arrived at the perfection of every detail of his works, as a matter of honour, alike for the interest of his employer and for his own reputation.'

Hamilton compiled an exhaustive survey of the measurements of every public stairway in Edinburgh to answer his critics.

No one felt the frustration over the delayed opening of the National Gallery more than Secretary Primrose, who had his own grounds for grievance. His salary had been fixed for the previous incumbent in 1840 and he felt that the building of a gallery which cost £50,000 could not be considered as a normal addition to these duties. In the course of a long Minute on this injustice it further emerged that there had been a cover-up:

'In consequence of the delicate state of health throughout of the late Mr Playfair the Architect, who died before the building was finished, the work devolved on me. I should be most loth to do this or have it supposed for I could not but share the wish of every member of the Board, of the whole profession of Architecture and in truth every person in Edinburgh that Mr Playfair, who had so ably planned the Buildings and decided all the means for overcoming the peculiar difficulties incident to its erection, should have his name alone connected with it as its architect and therefore during his declining health and with the prospect of a fatal termination, I had most sincere satisfaction in giving all the co-operation in my power to prevent any disappointment either to himself or to the public in this matter, and to ensure that the National Gallery should go down to posterity as his individual work.'

Playfair's death certificate, dated 19th March 1857, records 'Paralysis with probable softening of the Brain which continued several years' but one obituarist, John Murray Graham, maintained that his mental faculties remained unimpaired to the end. It is certainly true that the later Gallery drawings show a breakdown in his meticulous office routine. By May 1854 it is pathetic to see that he could not even write his signature in a straight line, and subsequent drawings, presumably by Hamilton, went out unsigned. On the other hand almost every detail of the building had been finalised before 1853 when he was first stricken by his illness.

The Treasury Minute governing the opening of the National Gallery was issued on the 25th February 1858. The long delay reflected the complexities of the task and the detailed arrangements betray a very thorough examination of every aspect of the Board's operations. £1,242 was reckoned to be the cost of running the new building, the burden of which was to be borne from the Board's own funds. To a certain extent the new costs were to be met by savings elsewhere. It was deemed that the official promotion of art through a National Gallery rendered redundant the grant and accommodation made available to the Royal Institution for the Encouragement of the Fine Arts in Scotland. For the 'beneficial and harmonious working', their Lordships thought it 'fair and reasonable' that the Curator should be selected by the Board from a list of four Members submitted by the Royal Scottish Academy. The new National Gallery's collections were to be provided by an amalgamation of the art collections of the Royal Scottish Academy, the Royal Institution, the Torrie Trustees; the Board's own reference material used in teaching; the National Association for the Promotion of Fine Arts in Scotland, whose pictures were purchased specifically for a National Gallery, and the pictures given or lent by private individuals. When displayed in Playfair's new building the Treasury felt confident that it would provide for 'the inhabitants of Edinburgh opportunities, which cannot be overestimated of rational amusement, mental cultivation and refinement of taste'.

Although the bodies whose grants were being cut were less than joyful, so far the Treasury's recommendations had seemed reasonable. The most far-reaching implication of their review, however, was their determination to transfer the Board's educational activities to the Department of Science and Art. Since the Department was responsible for art training throughout the entire British Empire (including Dublin) it was felt that Scotland had no right to be treated differently. The 'independence' of the Board's educational system was dismissed as 'isolation'. This information was ill-received by the Scots and it would have been difficult for the Treasury to have found a more tactless mode of expressing its views. Messrs. Cole and Redgrave were despatched from London to explain the attractions of the English system but throughout the spring of 1858 the Board held a number of abortive meetings to discuss the matter where tempers were probably too high for constructive debate. Sadly, the nationalists lacked the sort of effective leadership that Lord Rutherfurd might have been able to supply. A unanimous front proved impossible to maintain because the members of the Royal Scottish Academy, whose 'due position' was enshrined in the Treasury Minute, had no desire to 'dissent'. An important factor in its acceptance was the Treasury's recognition of Secretary Primrose's grievance and, 'pleased with his zeal', his salary was increased to £300. Faced by the Treasury's absolute determination, which was bluntly expressed in the information that this was 'why they had paid for the National Gallery' in the first place, all opposition crumbled as Primrose steered them to an acceptance of the Minute.

The history of the National Gallery illustrates the extent to which power was being centralised in Victorian Britain in a process that was intolerant of local idiosyncrasies. The building of the Royal Institution, by contrast, had been the result of a direct petition to the King from his Scottish subjects. The provision of a Scottish National Gallery was fiercely debated in the British Parliament, where the view was expressed that Edinburgh was no more deserving of financial support for such an institution than the great manufacturing towns of the Midlands.

If the Gallery was the cause of a momentous change in the organisation of art education, the Minute also required alterations to that building. To bring Scotland into line with England, responsibility for life drawing was to pass to the Royal Scottish Academy. Although teaching had long been one of their aims, the Academy's precarious foothold in the Royal Institution building had meant that this could only be a pious hope. Hamilton was therefore instructed to accommodate the necessary classrooms, and the completion of this task became the timescale for opening the National Gallery. Since Playfair's design was short on vacant space it is greatly to Hamilton's credit that he identified an ingenious solution. By providing a mezzanine floor in the north porticos, a life-room was created over the Royal Scottish Academy's hall with a classroom over that of the National Gallery. A staircase was contrived in Playfair's spinal corridor, but the problem was made more ticklish by the need to give the female model her own private entrance. Hamilton estimated that this work could not be completed by Christmas 1858, which had been the first target for opening the National Gallery. At the same time a chimney-piece in the National Gallery's southernmost octagon was removed. This had been provided so that the room could be used as a 'Council Room' – presumably by the Board itself. The chimney-piece was carefully dismantled for use by the Society of Antiquaries during their move to the Royal Institution's galleries.

THE GALLERY INTERIOR

A sub-committee was appointed to open the National Gallery. W. B. Johnstone RSA was appointed Curator and immediately identified a studio in the mezzanine of the west portico where he could restore pictures, and a chimney-piece, which still remains, was added for his comfort at modest expense. The task of the Committee and the Curator was largely confined to hanging the paintings because the Galleries were structurally complete. Since the National Gallery collection was an amalgam, there was no hope of achieving a unified framing scheme even if the money had been forthcoming, and Johnstone was to find it difficult enough to wring permission for cleaning from the varied owners. The hanging problem was exacerbated by a series of generous gifts which were attracted by the excitement of the new Gallery. In a moment of *élan* in 1851, Sir John Watson Gordon had offered to paint the portraits of the Academy's heroes: Messrs. Gibson Craig, Rutherfurd, Cockburn and Sir William Johnstone, late Lord Provost of Edinburgh. A portrait of Sir John Shaw Lefevre was also held to be essential in view of his distinguished contribution. Other Scottish artists responded with similar generosity and David Roberts' seven by fourteen foot canvas of Rome was a sure test of the size of the entrance doors.

If the exterior of the Gallery, as a result of the tight budget, appears to modern critics to be a purer work of the Greek Revival than Playfair intended, and the missing cupolas have had no admirers, it would be wrong to dismiss the austerity of the interior solely as the product of the Treasury's cheese-paring. Although it seems bafflingly plain in comparison to other High Victorian galleries like Barry's Manchester, when seen in its Edinburgh context it can be read as an example of rational design which was a dominant aesthetic in the 'Modern Athens'. The structural rationalism of the interior with its bare planks received an appropriately rational decorative scheme.

In Edinburgh the personification of rational decoration was David Ramsay Hay [Fig. 18], 'the first intellectual house-painter'. A protégé of Sir Walter Scott, for whom he decorated Abbotsford, Hay was one of the first painters in

18. D. R. Hay (1798-1866) with his dog Brush

1. Interior of the National Gallery in 1883.
Watercolour by Arthur E. Moffat (active 1880-93)

2. Proposed scheme for the interior of the National Gallery,
c. 1937-8. Oil sketch by Stanley Cursiter (1887-1976)

3. Interior of the National Gallery, c. 1867-77.
Looking into the centre octagon

4. Interior of the National Gallery in 1888, the western suite of rooms,
looking towards Benjamin West's *Alexander III Saved from the Fury of a Stag*

Redecoration 1987-8

5. Room A4 looking through
to A3, with Baerentzen's
The Winther Family
on the left and Raeburn's
*Reverend Robert Walker
Skating* beyond

6. Room A5

7. Room 10

Britain to apply recent advances in colour theory and aesthetics to his practice and his ideas were enthusiastically taken up by the citizens of the 'Modern Athens'. He was appointed contract painter to the Board and no Scottish architect patronised him more enthusiastically than Playfair who, with his dislike of lowest tender contracts, would simply inform his clients when their building reached a certain stage that Mr Hay would be calling. Although Hay began with the contract to paint the railings round the Gallery, in the confusion caused by Playfair's illness and the imminent bankruptcy of the Building Fund, the paintwork was actually carried out by Ballantine and Allan, whose firm was more celebrated for stained-glass. They were first employed by the Royal Scottish Academy to decorate their side temporarily, and in view of the financial difficulties it proved easiest to extend their contract to decorate the whole. Since, however, James Ballantine was a close friend of Hay's, and since the work was approved by Playfair, a 'scientific' scheme prevailed. Through practical experiment in his own and his clients' picture galleries, Hay had proved that a particular shade of 'purple' sometimes described as a 'claret' colour was the best medium for surrounding works of art and it was particularly sympathetic to the often damaged pigments of Old Masters. Although ideally Hay preferred to hang pictures against especially dyed cloth as he had done in the Hall of the Society of Arts in London in 1846, Playfair had obviously deemed this impracticable given the nature of the collections in the two galleries on the Mound [Fig. 19], both of which had

9. View of the Sir Walter Scott centenary exhibition held in 1871 on the Academy side of the building

to admit frequent changes. Whilst deep tones of crimson had long been fashionable as a background to paintings, the choice of this shade could now be justified in scientific terms since its effectiveness was partly the result of providing a direct contrast with the gilt frames. The cornices and surbases of the octagons were painted in imitation oak of a harmonising tone. Although 'graining' had come into disrepute in the south under the condemnation of Pugin and Ruskin, it remained in vogue in the 'Modern Athens' where Hay had raised the art to its highest pitch because the perfect imitation of natural materials was regarded as a scientific advance in house-painting. The surface of the coves was painted 'cream' to throw as much light onto the wall-faces as possible.

This scheme may have been a continuation of the way in which the Royal Institution's galleries were fitted up for temporary exhibitions since there is an account from Trotter, the Board's upholsterer, for hanging 'maroon cloth' on the walls and a matching drugget was also supplied [Col. pl. 1]. Sir John Watson Gordon may, therefore, have merely been selecting the 'tint' of the repeated colour rather than making a fresh choice as the Academy's Minutes superficially imply. The Academy had to pay for their own furnishings. Since seven hundred yards of carpet were needed for their new quarters, it is not surprising that their Minutes state they had 'with great care and deliberation chosen the pattern of the carpeting for the New Galleries'. Although Georgian taste had favoured the use of a single colour throughout a room, the selection of a green carpet to contrast deliberately with the red of the walls was in precise agreement with Hay's method of application of contemporary colour theory. Taylor, the Board's contract upholsterer who succeeded Trotter, charged £90 for the 'best Dutch carpeting'.

The Academy could supply the luxury of carpeting because, since they alone were permitted to charge for the annual exhibitions, they knew they could count on a polite audience. Since the Board, however, had pursued a policy of free admission (even in the Royal Institution), carpet was not an obvious choice but their Committee considered that its absence 'had a very bad effect'. Unwilling to bear full financial responsibility for so large a carpet, they put out tenders for its hire over three years which Taylor won at £35 per annum. Although the tenders were for 'red' carpeting, possibly a folk memory of the temporary fitting-up of the Royal Institution for special exhibitions, Taylor was asked to supply one which was identical in colour and pattern to that supplied to the Academy. Since this was a last-minute decision, it could not be ready in time, so for the opening the Board was lent the Academy's 1855 carpet, which had been superseded by a new one laid at the expense of the Art Manufacturers Association and which the Academy had subsequently purchased from them.

Not finding the painted linings of the new exhibition rooms a complete success, in 1855 one of the members, Thomas Hamilton, pressed the Academy to consider the purchase of sufficient cloth to drape behind the pictures so that no areas of painted boarding were left exposed. This is the arrangement shown in early photographs of their exhibitions. A similar concern for effect ruled in the other rooms fitted up on the Academy side and the 'Council stated that the library ought to be finished in rather a handsome style'. The table and fourteen chairs shown in a photograph of this room [Fig. 20] were supplied by Taylor in October 1856. Initially the room was laid with a drugget but the Academy aspired to a Turkey carpet which was to be added later.

On the western side, although the Board had stretched a point in the matter of carpeting, such luxury was impossible and the old mahogany benches and chairs from the Royal Institution galleries were moved across the road with the pictures. They were re-covered in 'red'. The similarities between the old and the new picture galleries were further underlined through their possessing identical interior porches built out from the linings of the first room. Playfair's design for the Royal Institution had distinctive octagonal glazed panels in the doors which were copied in the National Gallery. Old photographs of the benches show that some had been especially shaped to fit the octagonal form of the Royal Institution's galleries. A large set of them remains today in the Royal Scottish Academy. The chairs must have been supplied in the early 1830s to the enlarged Royal Institution and, interestingly, are a slightly cheaper variant of a set made to Playfair's own

full-size designs for the Royal College of Surgeons in 1832. Based on a standard Trotter New Town dining chair, but with flourishes of leaves supporting the back rail instead of a pair of capitals, they are another example of how Playfair could turn something quite ordinary into a powerful design.

A round table was also brought over and placed in the centre of the gallery. This was not judged a success and Taylor was asked to supply the centre sofa which is prominent in all early views of the interior. It cost £36 15s.; its step was shaped to suit 'the hot water apparatus' and it was covered in 'Turkey maroon cloth'. A new showcase for the Torrie marbles designed to fit into one of the octagons was a more substantial item. The Board's fear of extravagance led them to suggest that the cost could be cut if the front were made of two small, and therefore cheap, plates of glass instead of one large expensive one. To this unworthy suggestion Taylor protested that the price quoted 'was the very lowest at which he could make it' and that 'if 2 plates were used it would save only 21s. while it would totally spoil the effect'. The deep red of the walls and green carpet in the galleries were enlivened by notes of 'crimson'. The truncated obelisk stands for sculpture may have been already painted this colour in the Royal Institution Sculpture Gallery. The crimson guard ropes were spliced to seaworthy standard by seamen from the Fisheries Board. The hall was fitted up in oak and Taylor was asked to supply 'Furniture for the entrance hall consisting of Railing, Ticket taker's stand, Umbrella stand and Table'. None of these items, nor the '3 leather porters covered-in chairs' which were to be sent 'immediately' survives.

The formal opening of the western galleries took place on the 22nd March 1859 and could not have been more modest. At the Board's meeting on the 4th March to finalise its plans a letter from D. O. Hill was read 'deprecating the idea of opening with an evening promenade and moving consideration to have a Day of Ceremonial with speeches which he strongly recommended'. Doubtless still conscious of the Treasury rebuke at the extravagance of the foundation ceremony, the Board remained unmoved and Secretary Primrose had 1,500 tickets of suitable plainness printed, inviting the recipient in the name of the Board of Manufactures to 'A Private View of the National Gallery collection on Monday, the 21st inst. from 1 to 5 o'Clock.'

Today the Gallery seems almost as natural a feature of the centre of Edinburgh as the Castle rock. It still fulfils its original purpose admirably, although successive Keepers tried to keep in step with fashions elsewhere through the introduction of superficial decorations. Since the day it opened, however, nobody has ever sought to trifle with the exterior, and the New Wing of 1978, sunk deep below the surface of the ground, is a tribute to the finality of Playfair's solution to the problem posed by his 'beloved Mound'. In the light of its history the National Gallery can be seen as a fitting monument to the Board's first century of earnest endeavour in the promotion of Scottish art since the foundation of its Drawing Academy in 1760, just as it also marks the passing of that spirited independence. In spite of all the trials and the shortage of money, one of the greatest works of art in the care of the National Gallery of Scotland is surely the building itself.

[II]
A BRIEF HISTORY
OF THE NATIONAL GALLERY
AFTER 1859

Timothy Clifford

On the evening of the 24th March 1859 a dress reception was held by the Royal Scottish Academy in the whole of the new building that housed both the Academy and the National Gallery. The *Edinburgh Evening Courant* (26th March) estimated the assembled company at 2,000 or more.

'The galleries were decorated with graceful festoons and wreaths. Ornamental vases filled with the most fair and beautiful flowers were placed at intervals along the rooms, and a pretty floral device, surmounted by a crown, with the royal initials underneath, was suspended from the arch of the central octagon. The band of the 16th Lancers, stationed in the Academy's division, and that of the Sussex Militia in the National Gallery, performed in a charmingly subdued manner during the evening, a selection of operatic gems and chamber music. The scene, as the vast assemblage swept through the magnificent suite of rooms – the brilliant dresses of the ladies contrasting with the sombre evening costumes of the gentlemen, and the general effect enlivened by a sprinkling of scarlet uniforms – was of the gayest and most dazzling descriptions.'

Much has happened in the National Gallery since that celebrated evening and what follows concentrates on the architectural and decorative history of Playfair's building, undoubtedly one of the finest neo-classical structures in Scotland. The collections it contains, which have grown up over the past 158 years, have developed into something second only to Trafalgar Square in terms of public holdings. What the Gallery lacks in quantity it has always made up for in quality. Since 1946, it has benefited from the loan of thirty masterpieces from the collections of the Dukes of Sutherland as well as magnificent loans from other Scottish collections. The Gallery interiors since they first opened have been altered and modified to such an extent that by the 1980s they had become unworthy of the exterior and the collection inside [Fig. 21]. It has been the recent ambition of the Gallery's Board of Trustees to return these interiors to something of their appearance during their heyday, and to display the collections along more appropriate lines, following the aesthetic ideals of Playfair and Hay. All of this must be a reinterpretation, for we now use sophisticated security devices, the most modern lighting techniques, ultra-violet filters to limit the injurious effect of day-light, air-conditioning, and laser-printed labels mounted in perspex – all technological developments unheard of in Playfair's day. The overall plan is based on historical accuracy, however, and it is perhaps of use to explain our reasons for what we have done now and, at the same time, provide an historical context for our decisions.

In March 1859 300 pictures were hung in the suite of six rooms allocated to the National Gallery, while the Royal Scottish Academy in their section, and

21. Room 10, 1980s

with a similar wall area, hung some 850 pictures. The western galleries were
the National Gallery's property while the eastern galleries were the
Academy's. It would be quite wrong to assume that the Gallery's collection
was at that time of little consequence for it already contained many pictures
of real importance including the 26 bought on behalf of the Institution in
1830-31 in Genoa and Florence by the landscape painter Andrew Wilson,
partly on the advice of Sir David Wilkie. This acquisition, the nucleus of the
Nation's collection, was only six years after John Julius Angerstein's
collection was bought to found the nucleus of the London National Gallery.
Perhaps the finest canvas was the splendid *Lomellini Family* by Van Dyck,
but there were also two other magnificent Van Dycks of *St Sebastian Bound
for Martyrdom* and the full-length *Portrait of an Italian Noble*. Other capital
works included Paris Bordone's *Venetian Woman at her Toilet*, Jacopo
Bassano's *Portrait of a Gentleman*, Guercino's *Madonna and Child with St
John* and his *St Peter Penitent*, and works by Paggi, Cambiaso, Scorza, Furini,
Weenix, and Van Delen. The Academy in 1829-30 had acquired, as works of
modern art, the vast *Judith and Holofernes* triptych by William Etty, then
regarded as a triumph of the contemporary historical style. Later, but before
the 1859 opening, the Institution and the Academy between them had
acquired other great pictures including Tiepolo's vast *Finding of Moses* (1845),
his *Meeting of Anthony and Cleopatra* (the same year), Jacopo Bassano's
Adoration of the Magi, then believed to be by Titian (1856), Zurbarán's
Immaculate Conception and Gainsborough's glorious full-length of *The Hon.
Mrs Graham* (1859). Over and above this were all the fine pictures, marble
sculptures, vases and bronzes on loan from the Erskine of Torrie bequest to
the University of Edinburgh, which were placed on long loan to the Board of
Manufactures in 1845, and remained with the Gallery until they were
returned between 1955 and 1983.

The pictures were hung in two separate sections, the 'Ancient Masters' that
included works by foreign artists of all periods and the 'British Artists' of all
periods, but no other subdivisions were attempted. The opening of the new
Gallery was a catalyst to further gifts and bequests, the most notable being
the bequest of Lady Murray of Henderland of 1861 which comprised the

46

collections of Allan Ramsay the painter and his son, General John Ramsay. This included not only many oils and drawings by Ramsay himself, but the ravishing portrait of his second wife, and oils by Watteau, Lancret, Pater, Boucher, and Greuze. Such a quantity of fine pictures required galleries of appropriate elegance to display them.

The Gallery originally consisted of two parallel suites of three top-lit octagons linked by round-headed arches. Access to the two suites was from twin Ionic porticos to the north through rectangular entrance lobbies and galleries. In the centre of the building there were two lesser octagons and these were pierced by doors for access to both the Gallery and the Academy. Judging from the earliest painted image of the Gallery interior of c.1867-77 [Col. pl. 3] and from the 'archaeology' of recent building work, the flooring consisted of broad floorboards running in sections the length of the building and these were covered in green 'Dutch weave' carpet. The timber skirting had been oak grained, as also the bold plaster cornice. The cornice in the Academy half was grained in two tones, the lower zone being darker. The walls were clad, and indeed are still clad, in rather coarsely finished pine boarding, painted a dark shade of red. Later, probably in the late 1870s, this layer was lined with cartridge paper and painted a paler shade of red. By 1883 the walls were covered in maroon felt and the old green carpet had been replaced with a blue one as is shown by a dated watercolour by Moffat [Col. pl. 1]. In 1911 it was covered again with a 'scrim' painted maroon (while beneath the arches the walls were painted brown). In 1930 the Gallery walls were redecorated with a similar maroon base colour but overlaid with generous splashes and spatters of black and gold, to imitate a Japanese lacquer effect. Again, judging from our earliest painted image of the interior the sculpture stood on almost geranium red pedestals of truncated obelisk form and these contrasted, strongly and intentionally, with the darker and richer red behind. The two clashing reds were foiled by the green of the carpet while small objects, like glass-paste medallions by James Tassie, were displayed in mahogany cases with glazed, pedimented tops supported on turned legs. This combination of colours, fabrics, and textures, rich but austere, was typical of the style of David Ramsay Hay, who merited the contemporary soubriquet of 'the first intellectual house-painter'. This was an example of his scientific colour theories balanced with mathematical certainty. Here he demonstrated the superiority of his established principles of harmonious colouring in place of 'mere taste'. In 1850 Hay had already experimented with similar combinations of claret and green for Prince Albert's drawing-room at the Palace of Holyrood. Significantly, he had already laid down his *credo* for wall-hangings for pictures in an article published in the *Journal of the Society of Arts* (16th December 1846):

'In planning, therefore, the mode of decoration, his first object was to bring out the true and natural effect of the pictures. This has been effected by surrounding them with cloth of a deep purple hue, which colour is the most effectual in giving clearness to works of high art, such especially as may have suffered from imperfect pigments employed by the artist; . . . The adoption of cloth instead of painting upon the walls was suggested from the fact that the nature of its surface is rather to absorb than reflect the rays of light that fall upon it, and consequently to give greater effect to the pigments employed by the artist. The spaces of wall which surround the pictures will thus have the effect of being in shade, while the pictures themselves will appear in full light.'

The Gallery was at first furnished sparsely. Professional artists and amateurs, who came to copy the pictures three days a week, sat on solid

2. Chair in the National Gallery

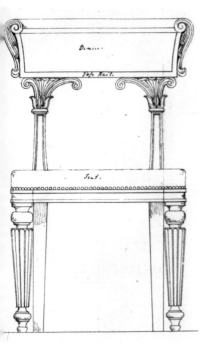

3. Design for a chair t the Royal College of Surgeons, y W. H. Playfair

grey-painted timber boxes pierced with holes that served for carrying handles. A few of these robust pieces of furniture that appear in the early views of the Gallery [Col. pls. 1, 3] still survive. Down in the present offices two suites of furniture are to be found from the earliest years of the new building, if not from the old Institution building next door. One set consists of six mahogany chairs with shaped rectangular backs terminating in scroll backs, and the other, a set of eighteen mahogany side chairs and two arms, their moulded cresting carved with paired honeysuckle motifs [Fig. 22]. The former set is very similar to those designed in 1832 by Playfair for the Royal College of Surgeons in Edinburgh [Fig. 23].

The arrangement of a series of red enfiladed rooms linked by round-headed arches goes back at least to George Dance II's Boydell's Shakespeare Gallery of 1788-9 [Fig. 24] which, in the early 19th century, became the British Institution's Gallery [Fig. 25]. This much frequented Gallery, so well known

24 (*left*). Boydell's Shakespeare Gallery in 1802.
Aquatint by Rowlandson and Pugin

25. *View day at the British Institute.* Oil-sketch
by Sir David Wilkie (1785-1841)

to Wilkie, must directly have influenced Playfair. He would also have been familiar with the very similar interiors devised by Sir John Soane for Dulwich College Picture Gallery of 1811-14 [Fig. 26]. It should not go unnoticed that Soane was a pupil of Dance. Red walls for pictures were the norm and appear to have been so since the red walls of the tribuna of the Uffizi in late-16th-century Florence. Most country house pictures were hung against shades of red damask in the 18th and early 19th centuries. Nash used maroon for the picture gallery at Attingham, Shropshire, in 1805-7, as did the painters Benjamin West and J. M. W. Turner for their own galleries.

Red is not only a rich and striking foil for gilt frames but, as Hay noted, intensifies the colours of the paintings themselves. At Edinburgh the red-painted, timber-planked walls, just like those in the 'Great Room' of the Royal Academy at Somerset House, were originally left uncovered by textiles. Pictures then were closely hung with frames touching, as if pieces of a massive jigsaw puzzle. Hung above them were swathes of red fabric tied at the top in loops with bunches of cloth ('choux') just as in the watercolour by George Scharf of the *Interior of the New Society of Painters in Watercolour,* 1834 [Fig. 27]. This type of arrangement persisted in the Gallery building until the late 19th century [Fig. 28]. The original cloth hangings at the Institution were supplied by the Edinburgh cabinet-making firm of William Trotter who also may have provided some of the furniture used in the National Gallery.

The National Gallery's collection of pictures grew to such an enormous extent that the Scottish National Portrait Gallery was founded in 1882, to open in a splendid Gothic Revival building in Queen Street in 1889. Soon

26. Interior of Dulwich College Picture Gallery, 1811, designed by Sir John Soane (1753-1837). Watercolour by J. M. Gandy (1771-1843)

27. *Interior of the Gallery of the New Society of Painters in Watercolours, Old Bond Street. Watercolour by George Scharf (1788-1870)*

28. The Great Room: RSA Annual Exhibition, 1884

49

afterwards, in 1895, a new Curator at the National Gallery was appointed, and it was then thought timely to reorganise the over-crowded arrangement of works then displayed, especially as many of them were of dubious quality. Added to this, every spring three rooms of the Gallery's pictures had to be dismantled to accommodate the Academy's Summer Exhibition.

The lack of space on the Mound was becoming critical and the working situation intolerable for both the Gallery and the Academy. Eventually a Departmental Committee was set up to enquire into the administration of the Board of Manufactures in September 1902. This was under the Chairmanship of the Rt Hon. A. Akers Douglas, Secretary of State for the Home Department, and included, amongst its distinguished membership, Sir Walter Armstrong, then Director of the National Gallery of Ireland, and the connoisseur Sir John Stirling Maxwell. Their Report led to the National Gallery of Scotland Act of 21st December 1906, followed by an Order of 12th January 1910 that specified the changed use of the buildings on the Mound. Amongst other more minor details the Act and Order proposed that the Board of Manufactures, set up after the Act of Union in 1707, be replaced by a Board of Trustees for the National Galleries, and that the whole of the south Mound building be handed over to the National Galleries. The Academy, removed from their section of this building, were granted free tenancy for an indefinite period of the ground floor of the north Mound building with rights for use of the galleries on the upper floor for their annual exhibition and diploma shows, while the exhibitions otherwise held in the galleries were the responsibility of the new Board. In return the Academy transferred to the nation 79 oil paintings, six sculptures, and a large quantity of watercolours and Old Master drawings. The old Institution building was gutted and rebuilt internally for its new purpose by William Thomas Oldrieve (1853-1922), HM Principal Architect to the Scottish Ministry of Works, and the building became known as the 'Royal Scottish Academy'.

The National Gallery adapted the entire south Mound building for their future use, the works supervised by Oldrieve. He made access to the Gallery building by a central doorway to the north and adapted the twin doorways to the old RSA and National Gallery into windows. The architect created a low central hexagonal entrance hall, stressed by grey-green Iona marble pilasters and lit by a shaped oval balustraded oculus that pierced the ceiling and

29 (*left*). Room A1, photographed 1961 showing Oldrieve's oculus

30. Oldrieve's stairwell showing *La Défense* by Rodin (1840-1917)

coincided immediately below with an identically shaped lantern in the room above [Fig. 29]. That room, formerly used by the RSA for their life classes, was converted into a gallery at first used for the display of works on paper. It was linked to the entrance hall by a stylish elliptical staircase, with Crestola statuary marble stringing. The cast bronze rails and balustrading terminated at the ground floor at a pair of bronze tripods ornamented with chains hanging from snarling lion masks, while on the landing in a round-headed niche stood a piece of sculpture [Fig. 30]. Underneath the oculus used to stand the superb écorché bronze pacing horse from the Torrie bequest, now returned to Edinburgh University. The inner lobby opened by way of Swedish green marble arches to left and right into the panelled suites of galleries while the most northerly pair of rectangular galleries was converted into octagons. There were other alterations which can be best understood with reference to the new ground plan (see page 64). The carpets were finally got rid of and replaced by parquetry flooring, a walnut dado was added, while banks of radiators were installed down the centres of the galleries, nicely disguised by banquette seats covered in brown corduroy, in much the same taste as those supplied by Oldrieve to the new Academy building [Fig. 31]. The extensive new look, contracted by Oldrieve to Thorburn & Son, cost £12,280 and opened to the public on 3rd June 1912.

31. Gallery interior modified 1912, photographed in 1926

Oldrieve appears as one of the unsung heroes of the National Gallery. With immense skill and respect for Playfair's masterpiece and the Gallery's collections, he adapted the building to perform as a very handsome small picture gallery. His entrance hall now looks depressing with its blonde polyurethaned pine fittings, brushed chrome door furniture and plethora of modern signboards dating from 1968-70. During this period of redecoration many pictures were taken out of their original frames and displayed in 'slips'. Shortly an attempt will be made to reinstate the bones of Oldrieve's scheme, opening up the blocked oculus and niche and taking away the newer sections of timber handrail which were brutally added and which destroy the sweeping line of the staircase. The picture store behind the existing bookshop will be removed, and in its place will be an improved shop, while a lift for the disabled will be installed for access to the gallery above. The area opposite for

32. Entrance hall photographed
in 1965 showing Oldrieve's doorcase
and oculus

cloaks will be enlarged while, overall, Oldrieve's elegant 'neo-mannerist', 'first-quality British oak' doorways and detailing will be faithfully reproduced [Fig. 32].

Playfair's open, arched enfilade in the main Gallery meant that each room was exposed to its neighbours in one long, gently articulated space. In the 1930s high ceilings were not only going out of fashion, even for Old Masters, but were entirely inappropriate for works of modern art. The Board of Trustees debated this problem on 19th October 1936 and the then Director, Stanley Cursiter (1887-1976), came up with a solution that materialised in 1937-8. It was resolved that large pictures were to be hung 'on the line', while double hanging was still admissible for smaller pictures. Room dividers in the form of large Corinthian plaster columns (the capitals copied from the Monument of Lysicrates) were to be introduced complete with tall attics, their ceilings pierced by shallow domes. Cursiter was an excellent painter with a fine eye and evidently, from his numerous surviving watercolours and oils depicting interior perspectives with these projected columns, the innovation was very carefully considered [Col. pl. 2]. Presumably it then admirably fulfilled its purpose but more recently, with its ponderous architecture darkening and reducing in size and grandeur the lofty, finely proportioned galleries, it has not been considered such a success. After a great deal of debate it was decided by the present Board of Trustees to take down these columns, preserving their bases and capitals for possible re-use elsewhere, and to return the interiors to their pristine, Playfair lines.

A National Gallery of Modern Art had been founded and opened to the public in August 1960 at Inverleith House in the middle of the Royal Botanic Garden. The modern collection multiplied until, from sheer lack of space, it was again moved in 1983 to its new location in the former John Watson's School, Belford Road – another grand neo-classical building. The foundation of the National Gallery of Modern Art freed the Mound of all but a few of its pictures, sculptures, prints and drawings that dated from after 1900.

At the Mound the cult of 'modernity' in 1971-2 was, however, considered appropriate for a suite of five new small galleries which were built as an upper floor at the south end, thus radically reducing the height of Playfair's two

33. Staircase to Rooms A2-A6, built 1971-2

34 (*right*). Rooms A3 and A4, 1971-2

most southerly octagons. The rooms were approached by an oval staircase with the treads of the steps covered with grey pigs-bristle carpet attached by metal strips and rubber nosings. The handrail of bright yellow spruce matched the staircase well and the Wedgwood-blue fabric of the walls was lit by a chandelier consisting of thirteen light bulbs suspended at different heights, all in globe shades [Fig. 33]. The floors were covered with grey Heuga-felt carpet squares, the walls, shorn of skirtings and cornices, were hung with coarse tweed, doors had flush finishes and brushed chrome fittings while the ponderous suspended ceilings penetrated the rooms like the bellies of airship gondolas. The utilitarian detailing still subscribed to the Festival of Britain, although built some twenty years too late [Fig. 34]. The space was in part created to house the great Maitland collection of French late-19th- and early-20th-century paintings, which had been presented to the Galleries in gifts of 1958, 1960, and the bequest of 1965.

Space has always been at a premium on the Mound and with the steady increase in the collections and staff, despite the existence of the Portrait Gallery and Gallery of Modern Art, it was necessary to find yet more accommodation. By excavating beneath the Gallery to the east this was brilliantly realised, inserting a new Print Room, Library, Picture Store and sequence of galleries. This subterranean complex, or 'New Wing', was opened to the public on 12th October 1978. The picture gallery space is devoted to the Scottish School, which is the largest single holding on the Mound, and it is also used for temporary exhibitions. However unsatisfactory certain aspects may be, the Galleries could hardly operate without it. The Property Services Agency, who were responsible for the New Wing, earned three awards for it in 1979: the Civic Trust Award, the RIBA commendation for Scotland, and the Concrete Society special mention [Fig. 35].

[III]
A GUIDE TO THE PRESENT REDECORATION AND DISPLAY

Timothy Clifford

In the current cycle of works initiated by the Board of Trustees from the Property Services Agency and Crown Suppliers, the National Gallery's objectives are to restore the building to something of its former austere splendour, while at the same time displaying much more of the collections to their maximum advantage. The purist approach would have been to destroy all that was not Playfair, but this has not been followed; rather there has been an attempt to retain a palimpsest of all that has been good subsequently, while at the same time making maximum use of modern technology. Pictures have been hung not as they were originally, when the building first opened, in a crowded mélange from cornice to carpet, typical of the Romantic and antiquarian taste of the time, but rather in a more classical, symmetrical arrangement as one might perhaps expect to see when such pictures were displayed in the late 18th or early 19th centuries. Maybe it will be seen as a failure of nerve that the original source has not been quite so slavishly followed, but hanging tiny pictures a few inches from the floor, or allowing massive pictures to break the cornice, would be viewed by many today with considerable scepticism. Pictures originally intended to hang as overdoors are displayed accordingly, while large pictures, like the Raeburn full-length portraits, are fixed high up at the sort of height that we know from documents Raeburn originally intended. It is well to remember that most 'Old Master' pictures that we see nowadays in a gallery setting were, if secular, hung in rooms with high dadoes or above chimney-pieces, while if sacred were seen from below placed above an altar table, which itself was often approached by several steps. Pictures that can now be too often regarded as valuable 'specimens' representative of an artist's autograph style were created to perform sacred, social, historical, propagandist, or purely decorative rôles that can be overlooked today.

There are few more picturesquely situated galleries than those on the Mound. In front of the National Gallery facing Princes Street is the solid Doric temple of the Academy, beneath it the green sward and trees of East Princes Street Gardens and above, perched on a great rock, the lowering silhouette of Edinburgh Castle. There should be an electric air of excitement before one enters the building and it is the task of the National Gallery to try and maintain this excitement throughout the public spaces of the building. Such a picture gallery can be considered as an extension of the 18th-century British landscape garden, of the type of Stowe or Stourhead. There are vistas; there is variety; there is the Sublime, the contemplative, the unexpected, the diverting, and even an element of wit. Picture hanging is not a mechanical activity, but an art form.

The interiors have to be functional and flexible while, above all, the collections must be as well presented as possible with the needs of visitors properly provided. There is here a close parallel to the parade rooms of the great country house, for the public picture gallery is the heir to just this tradition.

The visitor enters W. T. Oldrieve's hexagonal hall – which is scheduled to be returned to its former glory. The oculus to the upper gallery will be pierced, so other visitors will be able to look down from above like the figures in Mantegna's *Camera degli Sposi*. Straight ahead is the elliptical staircase leading up to Room A1. As the staircase walls are curved they cannot take pictures satisfactorily but, like the south staircase, will be decorated with part of the collection of Albacini casts of antique busts, to which further reference will be made.

At the top of the stair in ROOM A1 will be housed all the collections from *c*.1300-1525/7, that is approximately from Giotto to the death of Raphael and the Sack of Rome. Confronting us will be the large Spanish 15th-century panel of *St Michael*, on the far left wall the great *Trinity* panels by Hugo van der Goes lent by Her Majesty the Queen, and, on the far right wall, the three Raphaels lent by the Duke of Sutherland. Snaking out towards these two memorable walls will be Northern Gothic and Renaissance pictures to the left, and Italian Gothic and Renaissance pictures to the right. The lighting system will be changed; there will be new wall and floor coverings chosen as an appropriate foil for the pictures of the period. Around the room there will be sculptures and cases containing prints, drawings, medals, bronzes and ivories of the period – as well as 'cassoni' (marriage chests) and 'sgabelli' (chairs with wooden seats and backs) – to provide another dimension to the pictures on the walls. As far as the wall covering is concerned, something simple and chaste (a pictorial equivalent of plainsong) is being considered which will set off particularly well the gold-backed 'primitives'.

Returning downstairs, at the bottom on the right (that is to the left as one enters the Gallery) is the new ROOM 1. This forms the first of a suite of galleries decorated in the manner of Playfair and Hay in 1859 with maroon felt walls and green carpeting, as has already been described. ROOMS 1 and 2 contain one of the strongest holdings of the Galleries, Venice in the 16th century, with its superb group of works by Titian, Lotto, Veronese, Tintoretto, and the Bassano family. The delicacy, sensitivity and introspection of the pictures that were in Room A1 are succeeded by a robust, generous and painterly magnificence. Off to the right is a smaller octagon, ROOM 3, felted in dark brown, the cornice partly gilded, and the floor laid with coloured marble, which caters for all the smaller pictures that would otherwise be dwarfed in the grand suite of rooms with their long vistas and lofty ceilings. This has become a princely cabinet with finely finished pictures like the Bacchiacca, Poppi, Calvaert, Bril and above all the two glorious Elsheimers. It is intended to contain cases of 'Wunderkammer' and 'Kunstkammer' objects – bronzes, ivories, perhaps even narwhal tusks and nautilus shells. Room 3 will require several years of careful collecting and it is hoped will benefit from some exquisite and curious loans. ROOM 4 is one of the grandest rooms in the building and contains the greatest 17th-century Italian, Spanish and French masterpieces – Domenichino, Guercino, Guido Reni, the Bernini bust, El Greco, Velázquez, Zurbarán, Poussin and Claude. Because it cannot be fitted in later, the great 18th-century Pittoni altarpiece of *St Jerome with St Peter of Alcantara* from Santa Maria dei Miracoli, Venice, has been hung here as a pendant to the *Raising of the Cross* by G. C. Procaccini. ROOM 5 is set aside for the silent contemplation of the great *Seven Sacraments* by Poussin (Sutherland loan), a cycle of sacred images in Roman settings. The entire room is meant to be an evocation of the Poussin interiors with its newly laid marble floor, drab walls, dimly glowing oil lamp (now converted to electricity), the seven pictures with newly regilded frames, and a central banquette seat carefully detailing the couch on which Christ reclines in the *Penance.* How fitting this arrangement is, just off Room 4 with the other Poussins and Bernini's bust of *Carlo Antonio dal Pozzo.* These Sacraments, when they belonged to Paul Fréart de Chantelou, were greatly admired by Bernini in 1665, and it was Cassiano dal Pozzo (Carlo Antonio's close relation) who commissioned Poussin's first set of *Seven Sacraments* (now mostly belonging to the Duke of Rutland), and who also commissioned the Edinburgh Bernini bust and the Poussin *Mystic Marriage of St Catherine.*

After the extreme seriousness of Room 5, ROOM 6 is more fresh and relaxed, devoted to large Dutch 17th-century pictures by Ruisdael, Hobbema and Cuyp – with blue skies, scudding clouds, trees in leaf, sultry golden summer days with dozing cows and ships with billowing sails. Looking across to the right one can enjoy the vista of Van Dyck's vast *Lomellini Family* in Room 9, devoted to 17th-century Flanders.

On towards the south end of the building is ROOM 7, that is usually hung with smaller 17th-century Netherlandish pictures, more befitting a private cabinet. Here the walls change to grey, which is meant to remind one of 17th-century Dutch interiors with their off-white plastered walls, the lines of nailing covered by maroon gimp to help establish a link with the previous suite of rooms. Another colour is introduced here, bottle green, for chair seats and ribands. This colour is not only one of the commonest for Dutch fabrics at that time, as has recently been discovered in 17th-century inventories at Leiden, but acts as a complementary colour to the maroon gimp. Room 7 is intentionally very flexible. The lighting can be lowered for showing graphic material. The room will also be used for hanging small temporary exhibitions. Downstairs visitors can see the Scottish collections of the National Gallery in the suite of galleries called the New Wing [Fig. 35]. The only recent change here is that the graphic display area is now devoted entirely to showing Scottish drawings, watercolours and prints while more masterpieces of Scottish art are displayed upstairs taking their rightful place

35. The New Wing

36. Prints and Drawings Gallery

in the grand historical sequence of European painting. The New Wing galleries contain a survey of Scottish paintings c.1650-1900, including selections of works by Ramsay, Wilkie, Raeburn, and McTaggart. The present space is, however, far from adequate for the definitive display of the Scottish collection.

Upstairs, returning into Room 7 the visitor enters through an arched corridor into ROOM 8, decorated in the same manner as the previous gallery, but dedicated to displaying, on a regularly changing basis, a small selection of the Gallery's 15,000 or so works on paper [Fig. 36]. This space can be cut off from the main suite of rooms by panelled mahogany doors now fitted into the width of the wall, like window shutters.

The view from Room 8 down the enfilade of galleries to the north is now one of the most spectacular, with the vista closed by the enormous canvas, the largest in Scotland, by Benjamin West of *Alexander III, King of Scots, Saved from the Fury of a Stag by the Intrepid Intervention of Colin Fitzgerald* [Col. pl. 4]. It is a particularly happy coincidence that ROOM 9 is hung with Rubens and Snyders, both major 17th-century influences on West's great Scottish image. Room 9 also contains certain large Dutch pictures that, because of their scale, would otherwise not fit in Room 6.

Tucked to the right, and easily overlooked, is the staircase up to ROOMS A2-A6. These rooms are devoted to the small pictures c.1710-1900 that would otherwise be dwarfed by the grand suites of the downstairs galleries. The staircase, newly painted to simulate stone, with its new mahogany handrail, stanchions, specially woven carpet, and bronze and gilt bronze 'Colza' lamp converted to electricity, is supposed to clear the palate of the maroon palatial

scheme downstairs [Fig. 37]. Up these stairs we enter as it were a private house containing a beautiful collection of domestic-size pictures, mostly French. On the stairs are a group of plaster busts after the antique by Carlo Albacini (active 1777-1807). This selection was bought by Andrew Wilson, on the advice of the great archaeologist Visconti, from Florence for the Institution in 1839 and has remained in store all this century. The busts have been cleaned, but not repainted, and fixed on plaster consoles cast from moulds made for the Bank of England in 1847 after the design of C. R. Cockerell. The manufacturer was George Jackson, now of Hammersmith, a firm founded in 1780 under the aegis of the Scottish architect Robert Adam. The carpet is taken from a combination of two mid-19th-century patterns possibly originally made by Richard Whytock of Edinburgh, but now by W. H. Mackay [Col. pls. 5-7]. The cast iron stanchions are copies from a mid-19th-century pattern common in the New Town. The profile mouldings around the openings at the top and bottom of the stairs are copied from those on the building's exterior cut in stone.

ROOM A2, at the top of the stairs to the left, is dedicated to small European paintings c.1710-1775. This mixture of Italian, French, English and

Scottish art works remarkably well, allowing some fascinating juxtapositions that would otherwise be impossible if pictures were hung according to school and not chronology. The walls are covered with pink fabric that picks up many of the pinks appearing in the pictures, and this room, like Room A3 and half of A4, has been furnished with appropriate contemporary furniture generously sponsored by John Menzies plc with the aid of a Government (BSIS) Award 1987. ROOM A3 is filled with pictures *c.*1775-1820, with the notable exception of Gainsborough's *Landscape with a View of Cornard Village* of the 1750s. The blue has been chosen as a foil to the predominant brown of these pictures with its obvious reminiscence of Schinkel's colour schemes in Berlin and Von Klenze's at Munich and Leningrad, dating from the second quarter of the 19th century. The seat furniture is Russian while the console table is Scottish with a Glen Tilt marble top, almost certainly made by William Trotter of Edinburgh; the rather different neo-classical styles link remarkably well together. ROOM A4 is devoted to paintings *c.*1820-60. The colour chosen for the walls is an emerald green, a colour common for both the First and Second Empire in France, and reflected in the upholstery appearing in *The Winther Family* by Baerentzen [Col. pl. 5]. The furniture is Biedermeier and of the correct period for the room. The vista through is to ROOM A5 with Sargent's *Lady Agnew of Lochnaw* [Col. pl. 6]. The blue of the walls reflects the silk appearing as the background to the Sargent portrait. The furnishing of this room and ROOM A6 have been most generously sponsored by TSB (Scotland), with a subvention from ABSA.

8. Room A5

As both rooms are hung with 19th-century French paintings (with the exception of the Sargent), it was thought appropriate to display here not only Louis XV and Louis XVI period but also 19th-century French Revival furniture and bronzes by Degas and a marble by Rodin. For Room A6 the colour scheme has been taken from the colour of the files lying on the divan in Degas' oil of *Diego Martelli*. It makes a gentle and sensitive foil for the great Impressionist and Post-Impressionist pictures in this room. Among the delights for the visitor are the vistas like that of three Gauguins framed by the archway into Room A6 or the great Camille Pissarro of *The Marne at Chennevières* with its distressed frame the same colour and texture as the table beneath, on which stands the clock also ornamented with key fret [Fig. 38].

39. Marquis of Stafford's Gallery, London, 1808

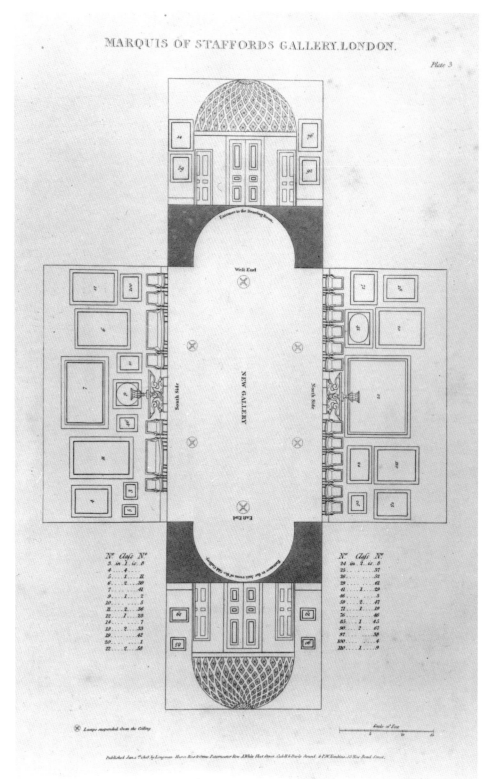

MARQUIS OF STAFFORDS GALLERY. LONDON.

Returning down the stairs we pass through Room 9 to ROOM 10, which houses the finest 18th-century pictures, including the enormous *Finding of Moses* by G. B. Tiepolo and *Achilles Lamenting the Death of Patroclus* by Gavin Hamilton. The latter has now been cleaned, relined and reframed. Around the walls is a suite of seat furniture stamped by J.-B. Boulard (1725-89), and two fine Louis XVI commodes with a matching pair of clocks [Col. pl. 7]. Coincidentally, the general disposition of pictures and furniture in this room corresponds quite closely with the arrangement of the Picture Gallery at Stafford House in 1808 [Fig. 39]. Many of the pictures in the National Gallery, now on loan from the Duke of Sutherland, were originally hung at Stafford House. ROOM 11 houses Wilkie's *Sir David Baird Discovering the Body of Sultaun Tippoo Saib* and opposite it, rather a disparate pendant, Frederic Church's *Niagara Falls*. It also contains three fine Turners (two on loan from Lord Rosebery), as well as Constable's magnificent *Vale of Dedham*. Standing on the tables in this room, and ROOM 12, are bronzes and hardstone vases from the Torrie bequest to Edinburgh University, recently loaned back to the National Galleries. Sculptures also stand on pedestals of truncated obelisk form painted geranium red, copied from those supplied in 1857-9. Raeburn's great full-lengths are hung here at much the same height that the artist originally intended. This explains why the artist has taken so much trouble over the painting of the foliage details in the foreground and the polished reflections from the sitters' boots and shoes, as these must have been intended to be at eye level [back cover].

ROOM 11 and ROOM 12 are in reverse chronological sequence, so that West's enormous *Alexander III Saved from the Fury of a Stag* can remain as the great vista picture on the north wall, fittingly surrounded by Raeburns. The present picture arrangement in the grand suite of rooms leaves many vast and distinguished pictures still unhung, including the Gallery's five great canvases by Etty, and enormous masterpieces by R. S. Lauder and David Roberts. Further accommodation must be found for many of these pictures and, in particular, those of the Scottish School.

The overall plan for the redecoration and rehanging of the National Gallery has been based on historical precedent. Taste and fashions change continuously, however, so no doubt what we have struggled to achieve will be altered again at some time in the future. Nevertheless, we hope the present redecoration will heighten our visitors' pleasure in an awareness of Playfair's splendid building, in which many of Scotland's greatest pictures are displayed.

FURTHER READING

Pictures for Scotland by Colin Thompson, published by the National Galleries of Scotland in 1972, provides an elegantly concise history of the complex development of the collection displayed on the Mound. Esme Gordon's *The Royal Scottish Academy 1826-1976* presents a lively account of the history of this sister institution with whom the National Gallery has shared the artificial hill and it gives the fullest available, and fittingly partisan, account of the quarrels which led to the foundation of the National Gallery. Both of these titles are out of print but in 1988 the latter author published the brief, but no less erudite, *The Making of The Royal Scottish Academy*. In the absence of a biography of Playfair, Ian Gow's essay 'William Henry Playfair Architect to the Modern Athens', published by The Scottish Georgian Society in *Pioneers of the Greek Revival*, 1984, is the only available account of both his professional and private life (available from the Royal Incorporation of Architects in Scotland's Bookshop, 15 Rutland Square, Edinburgh EH1 2BE). 'The Donaldson's Hospital Competition and the Palace of Westminster' by David Walker in *Architectural History*, Volume 27, 1984, supplies a very detailed and sympathetic account of the genesis of Playfair's masterpiece, whose convoluted history was a source of both professional satisfaction and personal vexation for its architect. *Master Class: Robert Scott Lauder and his Pupils* by Lindsay Errington, an exhibition catalogue published by the National Galleries of Scotland in 1983, includes the best available history of the Board of Manufactures' educational activities.

For the approach to picture hanging, reference should be made to 'Picture Hanging in Public Galleries', the Peter Le Neve Foster Lecture, given by Timothy Clifford at the Royal Society of Arts, 11th March 1987 (*Proceedings of the R.S.A.*, September 1987, pp. 718-34), and, by the same author, 'The Historical Approach to the Display of Paintings', *The International Journal of Museum Management and Curatorship*, 1982, I, pp. 93-106, and 'Some Considerations Regarding the Hanging of European Old Masters', *NA-CF News*, September 1983, pp. 32-7.

A NOTE ON SOURCES

The bureaucratic history of the National Gallery of Scotland is to be found in the records of the Board of Manufactures (Series NG) which are held in the Scottish Record Office. These include the Minutes of the Board (into which the Building Committee Minutes are engrossed) and the Secretary's outgoing Letter Books. The series also includes related and ephemeral material, but unfortunately the tradesmen's accounts have not been preserved. The most detailed documentation of the quarrels which led to the foundation of the National Gallery is to be found in the Minute Books of the Royal Scottish Academy, held by that body. With their keen sense of injustice the Academy's Minutes embody copies of much contemporary correspondence that does not survive elsewhere and cover much ground which the Board's records passed over in silence.

The primary source for Playfair's professional and private life is the long series of letters which he wrote to the Rutherfurd family, his closest friends, and which are among the Rutherfurd Papers preserved in the Manuscript Department of the National Library of Scotland. This collection also includes much relevant material, including the letter from Lord Cockburn quoted here. Playfair's drawings are preserved in the Special Collections Department of Edinburgh University Library and they include the designs for the four preliminary schemes. The 'client's' set of working drawings are among the Board of Manufactures papers in the Scottish Record Office. In addition, the Library of the Royal Scottish Academy holds Hamilton's discarded designs for the Mound and an important series of photographs of the National Gallery building beginning in 1860. The Department of Prints and Drawings of the National Galleries of Scotland possesses drawings by both Playfair and Hamilton. The Press Cuttings Albums of the Board of Manufactures were continued after 1907 by the National Galleries of Scotland who have retained the entire series, which provides both a convenient and invaluable source on many aspects of Scottish art.

National Gallery plan, 1906

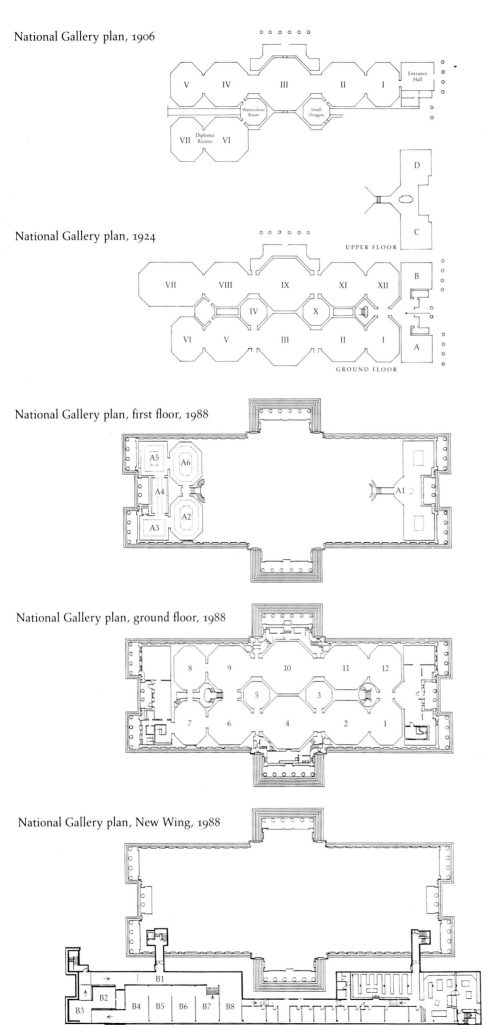

Room I: Dutch and Flemish Schools; II: French, Italian, German and Spanish Schools; Small Octagon: Foreign Schools; Second Archway: Dutch and Flemish Schools; III: British School; Third Archway: British School; IV and V: British School; Watercolour Room: Works in Watercolour and Black-and-White; VI and VII: Diploma Works of the Royal Scottish Academy. Sculpture placed throughout the Rooms.

National Gallery plan, 1924

UPPER FLOOR

GROUND FLOOR

(*Ground Floor*) Rooms I-VI: Foreign Schools; Rooms VII-XII: British School; Room A: Prints – Foreign and British Schools; Room B: Drawings – British School.
(*Upper Floor*) Room C: Drawings – Foreign Schools; Room D: Watercolours.

National Gallery plan, first floor, 1988

National Gallery plan, ground floor, 1988

National Gallery plan, New Wing, 1988

64